Courage of a Maltese Immigrant

Stories My Mother Shared With Me And More…

By

Rena Xuereb

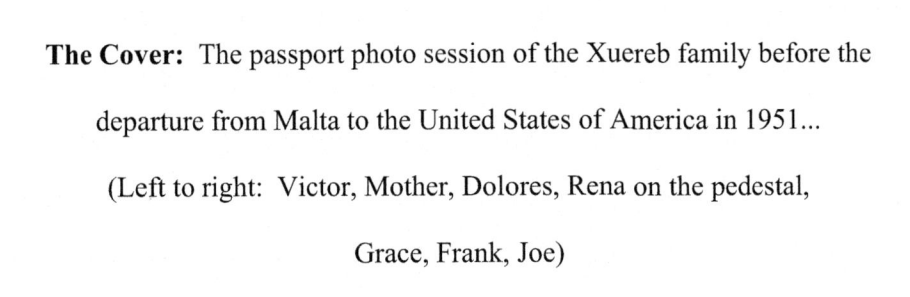

The Cover: The passport photo session of the Xuereb family before the departure from Malta to the United States of America in 1951... (Left to right: Victor, Mother, Dolores, Rena on the pedestal, Grace, Frank, Joe)

Copyright © 2024 by Rena Xuereb

All rights reserved. This book or any portion thereof may not be reproduced or used in any manner whatsoever without the publisher's express written permission except for using brief quotations in a book review.

Acknowledgments

A heartfelt thank you to my husband, children, siblings, nephews and nieces, extended family, and friends for their unwavering encouragement and support in uncovering the memories of our past. The information and stories you shared have transformed this book into a diary of dates, events, and captivating narratives. Your assistance has been both enormous and endless.

I would also like to extend my gratitude to the staff at the Public Registry in the Evans Building on Merchants Street in Valletta, Malta. They patiently responded to my inquiries and questions over several weeks and beyond.

My deepest thanks go out to the ever-knowledgeable employees at the National Archives in Rabat, Malta, housed at the historic Santo Spirito Hospital. They introduced me to a wealth of historical information and documents, tirelessly fetching records and details.

Special thanks to Dan Brock, who provided me with valuable dates, information, and unending encouragement, along with constructive criticism.

Charles Said-Vassallo significantly expanded my understanding of genealogy and offered tremendous help in tracing our family's history farther back than I ever imagined.

I'd also like to acknowledge Michelle Pisani-Paull, who was always ready at a moment's notice to assist with translations when needed.

It saddens me deeply that some of the individuals who provided stories and information have passed away before I could complete this book. I had hoped they would be the first to read it and share in the joy of their contributions.

Lastly, my sincere gratitude to my five children who helped and encouraged me daily. My son Joseph, who saw this book to the finish, putting up with all my questions and comments, and my Dominic for the beautiful book cover he created. I absolutely love it.

Foundling Wheel, where unwanted newborn babies were called "creature Gettate," meaning to throw away.

Note: In the center of this image lies the Foundling Wheel, a wooden revolving cylinder window located at the former Santo Spirito Hospital. Regrettably, in days gone by, many women would visit this window during the early hours of the day, hoping to remain unseen as they discreetly placed their infants inside and gave the wheel a gentle turn. This action would trigger the ringing of a bell to alert the staff. Tragically, these mothers would never see their newborn children again.

Courage of a Maltese Immigrant

Stories my Mother shared with me

and more...

By: Rena Xuereb

Email: rxuereb5@gmail.com

PREFACE

The following stories are dedicated to the living and deceased children of Josephine Gauci Xuereb, her grandchildren, great-grandchildren, great-great-grandchildren, and all generations to come. For those of us fortunate enough to have known her, we will never forget what a remarkable, witty, and courageous Maltese woman she was. For those who were born after her passing on January 6, 2003, or were too young to remember sharing a cup of tea with Nanna, as she was respectfully called, my hope is that as you read on, you will feel as though you have known her all your life.

In her last few years at Marycrest Manor Nursing Home (in Livonia, Michigan), alongside her youngest daughter, Rena Xuereb, and her grandchildren Maria Suchyta, Ana Victoria Campos, and Joe Suchyta IV.

My desire is for everyone to become acquainted with Nanna, the matriarch of our family, to read her stories and memories, to share her laughter, and to celebrate her life. It is my hope that you will enjoy these memoirs as much as I enjoyed the research, interviews, and the gathering of information needed to compile them. Those of us who share in these memories pray that these stories of Nanna will become a cherished family heirloom for future generations to take pride in their Maltese heritage.

Table of Contents

PREFACE 8
Introduction 13
Mother 16
Coming To America 17
Leaving Malta 20
Chronological Table Of Maltese History 31
Mother's Genealogy 32
Dolores 33
Josephine Gauci 34
Young Josephine 36
World War I 38
Josephine's Younger Years 40
Maltese Bagpipes 41
Mother's Schooling 42
Farmer's Hygiene 45
The Maltese Stamina/Faldetta And/Or Għonnella/Ċulqana 48
Francesca Borg Gauci (Our Nanna) 50
The Marriage 59
Feast Of St. Peter/St. Paul 64
Life On The Farm 65
Marija's Hernia 76
Drinking Petrol 78
Inheritance 79
The Three Brothers 80

Returning To Malta	81
Mom And Dad's Siblings	86
Jewelry	88
Laqam	89
Mosta	91
Father's Parents	93
Dad's Genealogy	94
Dad And School	97
Dad's Taxi, Bus, And Jeep	100
World War II	102
Marija And Joe's Marriage	104
Dad Going Back To Malta	106
Baby Boy	108
Ziju's Tragic Death	109
The Famous "Milsa"	111
The Farm Horse	114
The Maltese Cow	116
House On Bristol Street	118
Hanging Clothes In The Winter	120
Baker Street House	121
Saturdays	134
Reader's Digest	139
Measles And Chicken Pox	140
Abandoned House On Baker	141
First Shower	142
Mother's Health Problems	144
Grace And Joe	147

National Guard And Boy Scouts 157
Victor And The Franciscan Order 158
Sr. Carmela Xuereb RSCJ 162
The Fenech Family 164
Connie Zerafa 166
The Neighbors 167
Dad's Midlife Crisis 169
Year 1968 173
Department Of Immigration 175
Mother's Last Trip To Malta 177
Cousin Mary And Charlie Buttigieg 179
Mother In Las Vegas 187
Mother's Pets 188
Holy Redeemer And Friends 191
Dad's Death 193
Back In New York 194
In Conclusion 195
In Memory 199
Maltese Recipes 201
   Aljotta (Fish Soup) *202*
   Bigilla (Broad Bean Dip) *203*
   Bragioli (Stuffed Bundle Of Beef) *204*
   Brungiel Mimli (Stuffed Eggplant) *205*
   Froga Tat-Tarja (Pasta Omelet) *206*
   Gbejniet (Fresh Maltese Cheese) *207*
   Pastizzi Dough *208*
   Pizza Toast *212*

Ravioli *213*
Ricotta (Whey Cheese) *214*
Ross Il-Forn (Baked Rice) *215*
Soppa Tal-Armla (Widow's Soup) *216*
Minestra Tal-Haxix (Vegetable Soup) *217*
Stuffed Tal-Fenek (Rabbit Stew) *218*
Timpana (Baked Macaroni Pie) *219*
Torta Tal-Irkotta (Rikotta Pie) *220*
Torta Tal Laham (Corned Beef Pie) *221*
Maltese Sweets 222
Biskuttini Tal-Lewz (Almond Cookies) *223*
Biskuttini Tar-Rahal (Village Biscuits) *225*
Qaqhaq Tal Gunglien (Sesame Rings) *226*
Figolli (Easter Cookie) *227*
Galletti (Maltese Cracker) *229*
Imqaret (Date Filled Snack) *230*
Pudina Tal-Hobz (Bread Pudding) *232*
Qaghag Tal-Ghasel (Honey Ring) *233*
Xkunvat (Crumpets) *234*

INTRODUCTION

My name is Rena, short for Nazarena, the youngest of seven living children of John Xuereb and Josephine Gauci Xuereb, two amazing people, my heroes and mentors. Over the years, my siblings and I were told many stories by our parents about life on the Island of Malta, allowing for the passing down of numerous stories and lessons. The struggles during their childhood, farm life, the wars, and the final decision to leave their birthplace, their eldest daughter, and their siblings in Malta are just a few of these stories.

John Xuereb and Josephine Gauci Xuereb.

I have wanted to recount my parents' stories for several years, but I often asked myself, where do I start? Not knowing where to begin has prevented me from starting at all. I feared not having enough information and not doing justice to my parents' memory. I've never written anything of this nature and magnitude before, so I find myself reading more about the proper writing format, whether to write in the present or past tense and what to include or exclude.

My goal, at the very least, is to write these memories down on paper to share with my children, siblings, and their children. For years, I've had notes and short stories embedded in my head, going over them repeatedly to avoid forgetting any details of these memories and stories that have been stored in my heart for so long.

It is an honor for me to retell my mother's memories, her background, childhood, marriage, family, friends, and most importantly, her courage. I once heard someone say that if these stories aren't written down, they will be gone and forgotten forever. I thought about how sad and unjust it would be for Josephine Xuereb's courageous life story not to be told, absorbed, and passed on to others.

I have shared some of these stories with my children, nephews, and nieces, and their joyful, surprised reactions have encouraged me. I've mentioned to a few people, both in and out of the family circle, that I have all these memories and wonderful stories my mother has told me over the years and that I want to share them with others. Everyone has encouraged me to start writing, and I can't thank them enough, just as they can't wait to read these treasured stories. Each time, it has reinforced how important it is to get these stories permanently documented on paper for everyone to read and enjoy repeatedly.

✠✠✠✠✠

Now that I have begun the task of transferring these memories onto paper, I find myself obsessed with it. I think about my mom and dad every day, almost constantly. I find myself researching and writing stories down daily as they come to mind. Even though I am a novice at writing, I am truly enjoying this adventure. I am finding a sense of fulfillment in my mother's memory and hope I do her justice and make her proud. Most of all, I hope it will be a story everyone enjoys.

Mom and Dad   *Mother with her harvest*

Rena and Dad burning trash.

Grace, Rena, Dolores, and Dad

MOTHER

This is a memoir of my mother, Josephine, and I hope to capture her love and courage on paper as I write about her life. My Mother was a down-to-earth person with a gift for great one-liners. She was set in her ways but would do just about anything for you without inflicting or pushing her beliefs and ideas on you. Ginger McIntyre Xuereb, my brother Joe's first wife, the mother of his six children, and a treasured sister-in-law, pointed out so eloquently at Mother's funeral back in January of 2003 that Mother would never tell you what to do but rather put the information and advice out there in a way that you could understand and hopefully grasp and run with it. You know, I never stopped to think about that quality of my mother, but I instantly found myself going over incidents of my own life where I found this to be true. She was always there for you but never in your face. She was there if you needed her and needed a hand, but she was never there to tell you what to do or how to do it. That was my mother; these are her stories as I so proudly remember them.

Josephine Xuereb (age 76) in Malta 1985, sporting a Detroit Tigers cap on a Sunday outdoor shopping trip.

COMING TO AMERICA

I have to start these stories with my dad, John Xuereb. Leaving Malta was his idea; Mother wanted nothing to do with it. She was perfectly happy on her Island of Malta, surrounded by her family and farm, the place she loved. The 1950s saw a large number of people exiting Malta for a better life because things were becoming very difficult in Malta after World War II. Jobs were scarce, and Dad tried working in England, but that didn't work out. He wasn't fond of farming life and wanted something different. He was headed to Australia, but his nephew Joe Shuereb, who left Malta years earlier and was living in Detroit, wrote my dad and informed him that he could immediately obtain a job in the United States. That was it, that's all my dad needed to hear. He boarded a ship for the U.S.A. in August of 1950, leaving his family behind. Just a few months later, he notified my mother to join him. We left Malta in June of 1951, just ten months after my dad. During those agonizing ten months, Mother was non-stop trying to get everything ready for us to leave, which meant Mother and six children had so much to get done. Leaving her eldest daughter behind, thinking she'd never see her again. The following stories are about Josephine Xuereb, her courage, and her tenacity.

Kemm hawn nies fid-dinja.

How many people in this world? Or, literally, so many people in this world.

Dad's favorite saying.

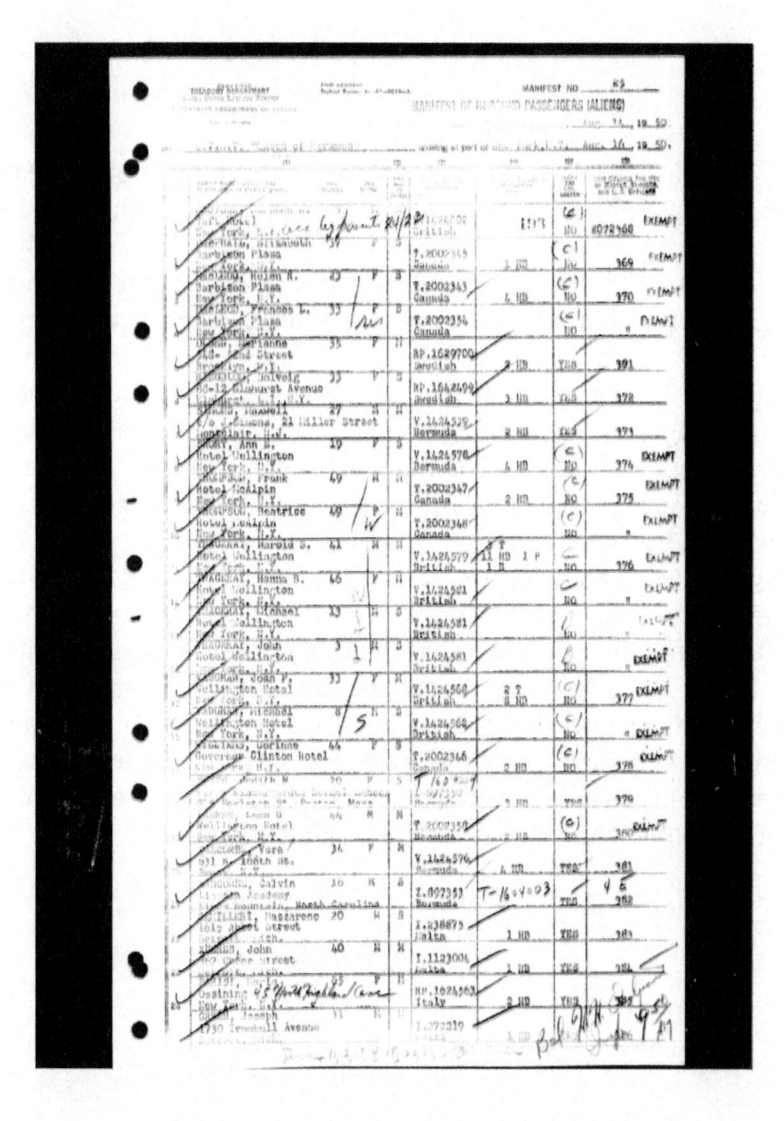

Dad's passenger list on the Queen of Bermuda (Dad third from bottom)

Dad's ship "Queen of Bermuda" that brought him to the U.S.A. in 1950.

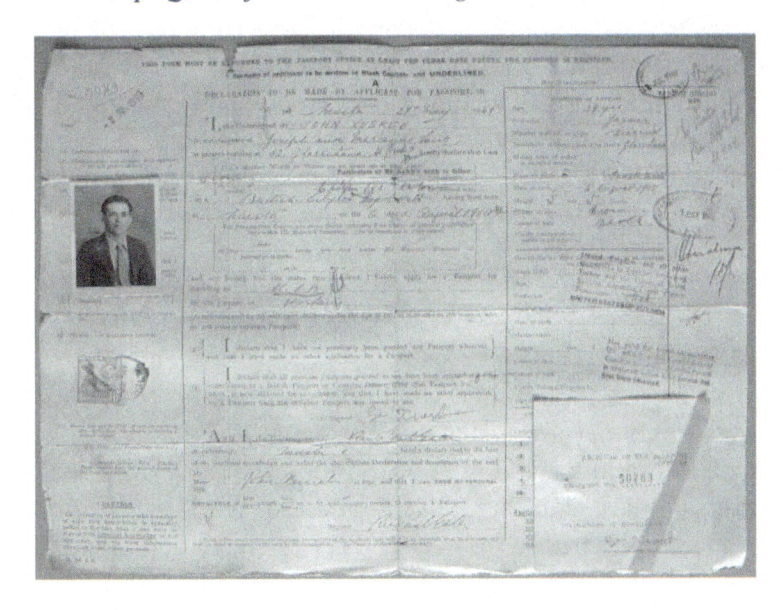

Dad's passport application in 1949.

LEAVING MALTA

The day finally arrived. This was the day Mother had prepared for and dreaded for months. The day she thought of time and time again, looking for every excuse not to go, not to leave Malta. Mother spoke about consulting with her parish priest, asking if she had to go and uproot her family to this unfamiliar place called America. His response kept echoing in her head for years: "You must follow your husband, if you don't follow him, you may be responsible for his actions." How she wanted the priest to say something more along the lines of: "No, if you feel you need to stay here, then do so." Hearing this time and time again as a young adult made me reflect upon a parish priest's power over his congregation; it was his powerful words of action that more or less decided if we left Malta or stayed. Well, that and big brother Joe's insistence. He takes credit for getting us to The United States of America, the big man who just turned 15 in April of 1951, just two months before our departure. He kept insisting and finally halfway convinced my mother that it was a better world. Several years later, Joe admitted that his wanting to leave Malta was selfish because, as a teenager, he heard America had hundreds of fair-skinned blond women to choose from.

✠✠✠✠✠

For years, we thought the voyage from Malta to New York took three weeks. Mother always stated that we left Malta just as I turned four (June 9th) and arrived in the U.S.A. on the feast of St. Peter and St. Paul (L-Imnarja) on the 29th of June. So, with that in mind, this would indicate the trip to be twenty days or so. In actuality, it was a 13-day trip, leaving Malta's Grand Harbour on the 15th of June and arriving at the Port of New York on the 28th of June. Mother often talked about my sister Grace, who was almost twenty, being seasick during the whole trip. Mother found the trip at sea rough at times as well but fought hard to keep strong and care for us rather than lay down and rest. Mother was so skeptical of everything and so protective of us that she would not let us eat the food that was offered on the ship, fearing it was poisoned. She finally broke down when we had to eat.

The total opposite of Grace was fifteen-year-old Joe, who was usually running around the ship chasing the girls, especially the fair-skinned blond ones. Mother said Joe claimed to have lost his gold ring on that ship, but she believed he probably professed his love to some blonde he just met. His testosterone was in full gear at fifteen, as my mother described it.

✠✠✠✠✠

Imagine going on a one-way family trip with six children, all the packing, all the headaches that go into taking a trip. So much had to go into our departure months ahead of this. Photos had to be taken; passports had to be obtained; ship vouchers confirmed. (We were originally headed for Australia, as you see on our passport application, but my dad changed course and decided on America.) Children's Passage was free for anyone Australia-bound, but now my mother had to scrounge up extra money for five minors (Grace was over 18 years of age). Mother sold everything on the farm she could. Now imagine this trip being a permanent one, that much more to remember and prepare for. Then, to top it off, imagine trying to do all this with a sick child. I was still recovering from my bout with milsa (spleen infection), which I will write about later. My mother would always point to our family photo (on the cover) that was taken before our departure. She would show me how she was clenching her fist in fear and anger, and then she would go straight to my image, the young child standing on the pedestal, pointing out the jaundiced color on my face and the distended belly I had. So much stress for any woman to bear on her own, let alone my mother. Our oldest sister Marija and her husband, Joe Gatt, along with two small boys, Salvu (Sam), who was just two, and Ganni (John), who was only one, would move from the farm up the road to our family farm located in what was known as Ghajn Rihana, the limits of St. Paul's Bay, just around the corner from the "Targa ta St. Joseph" (Step of St. Joseph) statue on the small hill as you left Mosta and near the small chapel of Santa Margerita. There, they tended to the farm chores that never ended. Shortly afterward, Marija's third son Gamri (John Mary), called Jimmy, would soon be born on the farm, known then to be 82 Burmarrad Rd. I understand my sister Marija did not see us off; I'm sure it was much too painful. I do not recall ever seeing any luggage or trunks; perhaps we used boxes, who knows. Mother brought the essentials for our trip: wool blankets, photos, clothing, memorabilia, and some food. Before taking a ferry to the actual enormous ship at the Grand Harbour M.V. Italia, Mother's oranges and other foods were confiscated; this did not start the journey off to a good beginning. Mother was so angry. In her mind, she felt we were going to a primitive country filled with diseases. After all, her birth island was the only home she had ever known. She never even ventured to the nearby island of Gozo on a small boat during her 42 years in Malta. I do not recall that day or the ship; remember, I just turned four years of age. Brother Victor, who just turned 11, reminded me that we had two adjoining cabins, and I can almost see them, but I don't know if they're just the stories I've heard over the years or the actual thing.

We thought we had arrived at Ellis Island, but honestly, the island was closed during that period. We arrived at the Port of New York Harbor, and after the tedious passenger clearing process, we boarded a train to Detroit, where Dad would be waiting.

✠✠✠✠✠

Can you imagine losing your nine-year-old son at the New York City train station? That's exactly what happened to us in this strange foreign land. Mother probably lost sight of Frank for a quick second, but the story lasted for years. It always started with, "The time we lost Frank in New York City...." Thank God he was found immediately. A police officer brought him over, and since none of us spoke English--actually, Joe managed a few words--we didn't know what the policeman said, but he could tell from my mother's pale, worried face that he was indeed ours. Mother would say, can you imagine Dad's face if we arrived in Detroit without his youngest son? I believe Frank stayed close by from then on.

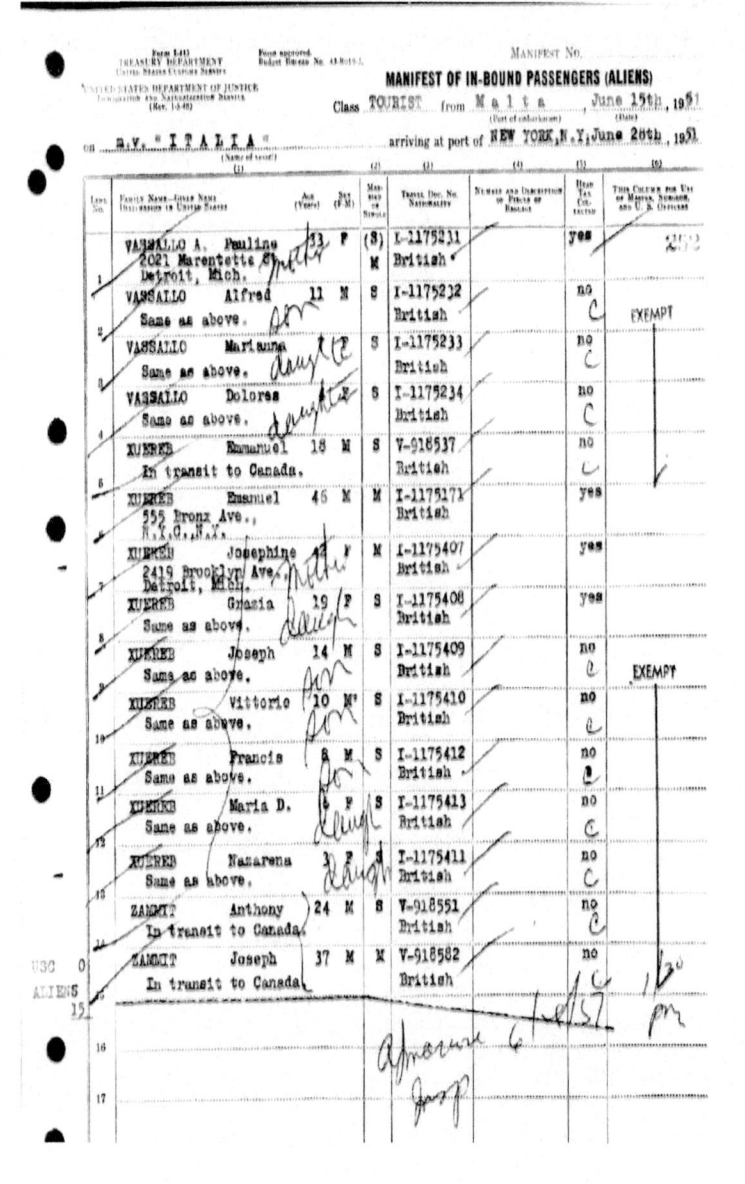

Line No.	Family Name – Given Name / Last Residence in United States	Age (Years)	Sex	Married or Single	Travel Doc. No. / Nationality	Number and Description of Pieces of Baggage	Head Tax Collected	
1	VASSALLO Pauline 2021 Marentette, Detroit, Mich.	33	F	(S) M	I-1175231 British		yes	252
2	VASSALLO Alfred Same as above.	11	M	S	I-1175232 British		no C	EXEMPT
3	VASSALLO Marianna Same as above.			S	I-1175233 British		no C	
4	VASSALLO Dolores Same as above.			S	I-1175234 British		no C	
5	XUEREB Emmanuel In transit to Canada.	18	M	S	V-918537 British		no C	
8	XUEREB Emanuel 555 Bronx Ave., N.Y.C., N.Y.	46	M	M	I-1175171 British		yes	
9	XUEREB Josephine 2419 Brooklyn Ave. Detroit, Mich.		F	M	I-1175407 British		yes	
	XUEREB Grazia Same as above.	19	F	S	I-1175408 British		yes	
	XUEREB Joseph Same as above.	14	M	S	I-1175409 British		no C	EXEMPT
10	XUEREB Vittorio Same as above.	10	M	S	I-1175410 British		no C	
11	XUEREB Francis Same as above.	8	M	S	I-1175412 British		no C	
12	XUEREB Maria D. Same as above.		F	S	I-1175413 British		no C	
13	XUEREB Nazarena Same as above.		F	S	I-1175411 British		no C	
14	ZAMMIT Anthony In transit to Canada.	24	M	S	V-918551 British		no C	
15	ZAMMIT Joseph In transit to Canada.	37	M	M	V-918582 British		no C	

MANIFEST OF IN-BOUND PASSENGERS (ALIENS)
Class TOURIST from Malta June 15th, 1951
m.v. "ITALIA" arriving at port of NEW YORK, N.Y. June 26th, 1951

The Xuereb family is listed toward the bottom of the page of this passenger list. Our nationality is listed as British because in 1951 Malta was part of the British Commonwealth.

M.V. Italia, the ship that brought the Xuereb family to America in 1951.

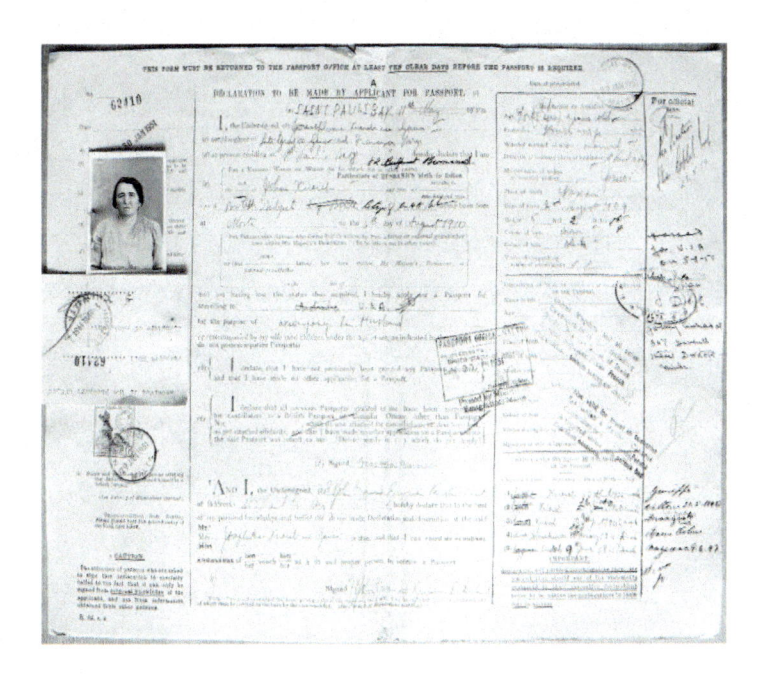

Mother's passport application with her five minor children listed in the bottom, right.

Grace's passport application, since she was 19, she had her own application.

The first family photo which was taken in America, in 1954. From left to right: Joe, Frank, Dolores, Victor, Grace, Mom, Rena and Dad.

Frank, Victor and Joe.

Rena, Dolores and Grace.

Back row: Frank, Victor, Joe. Front row: Rena, Grace and Dolores.

Dolores, Rena, Joe, Frank, Mother, Victor and Grace.

Marija, Grace, Joseph, Victor, Frank, Dolores, and Rena: the first photo of all seven Xuereb siblings during Marija and Joseph Gatt's 50th wedding anniversary.

In the back: Frank Xuereb. Middle row: Grace Xuereb Vella, Ginger McIntyre Xuereb, Dolores Xuereb Stone, John Xuereb, Joseph Xuereb, Victor Xuereb. Front row: Evelyn Debono Xuereb, Theresa Atkinson Xuereb, and Rena Xuereb.

Gail, Frank, Dolores and, standing, Joe.

Joe Shuereb and Donna Mclaughlin Shuereb.

CHRONOLOGICAL TABLE OF MALTESE HISTORY

Period	Phase	Date	Principal sites or events
Geological	Miocene	20 million y.a.	Formation of roc
		5 million	Malta an Island
	Pleistocene	100,000	Pygmy fauna
Neolithic	Ghar Dalam	5000 B.C.	First occupation; farming
	Grey Skorba		Stone implements; ornaments
	Red Skorba		East shrines
Temple Period	Zebbug	4000	Rock cut tombs
	Mgarr	3800	
	Ggantija	3600	Early temples
	Saflieni	3000	Hypogeum
	Tarxien	3000	Later temples
Bronze Age	Tarxien cemetery	2500	Cremation; metal use
	Borg in-Nadur	1500	Fortified villages; cart ruts
	Bahrija	900	Shaft and chamber tombs
Phoenician	Republican	750	Tombs; evidence of trade
	Punic	600	Ta' Slig temple
Roman	Republican	218	Cities
	Imperial	31	Villas, baths, tombs, Christianity
	Byzantine	330 A.D.	Catacombs
Arab		870	
Mediaeval	Norman	1190	Requested by Christianity
	Swabian	1194	Adoption of European traditions
	Angevin	1268	Local government
	Aragonese	1282	Oldest surviving churches
Modern	Knights of St. John	1530	Fortifications, auberges, churches
	French	1798	
	British	1800	Victoria lines, modernization
	Republic	1964	Independence

MOTHER'S GENEALOGY

Descendants of Silvestro Gauci

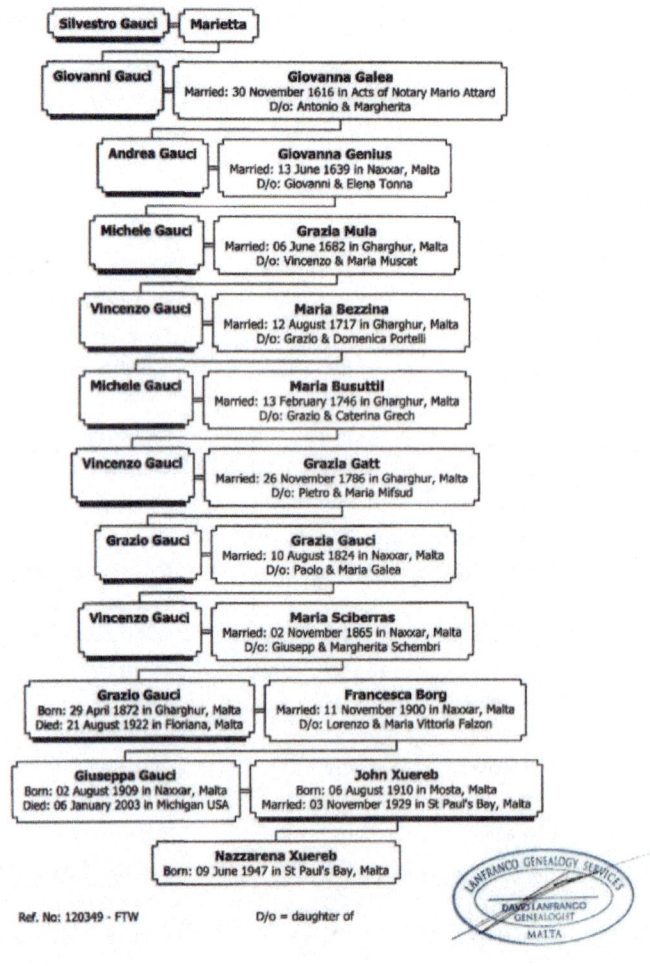

- **Silvestro Gauci** — **Marietta**
- **Giovanni Gauci** — **Giovanna Galea**
  Married: 30 November 1616 in Acts of Notary Mario Attard
  D/o: Antonio & Margherita
- **Andrea Gauci** — **Giovanna Genius**
  Married: 13 June 1639 in Naxxar, Malta
  D/o: Giovanni & Elena Tonna
- **Michele Gauci** — **Grazia Mula**
  Married: 06 June 1682 in Gharghur, Malta
  D/o: Vincenzo & Maria Muscat
- **Vincenzo Gauci** — **Maria Bezzina**
  Married: 12 August 1717 in Gharghur, Malta
  D/o: Grazio & Domenica Portelli
- **Michele Gauci** — **Maria Busuttil**
  Married: 13 February 1746 in Gharghur, Malta
  D/o: Grazio & Caterina Grech
- **Vincenzo Gauci** — **Grazia Gatt**
  Married: 26 November 1786 in Gharghur, Malta
  D/o: Pietro & Maria Mifsud
- **Grazio Gauci** — **Grazia Gauci**
  Married: 10 August 1824 in Naxxar, Malta
  D/o: Paolo & Maria Galea
- **Vincenzo Gauci** — **Maria Sciberras**
  Married: 02 November 1865 in Naxxar, Malta
  D/o: Giusepp & Margherita Schembri
- **Grazio Gauci**
  Born: 29 April 1872 in Gharghur, Malta
  Died: 21 August 1922 in Floriana, Malta
  — **Francesca Borg**
  Married: 11 November 1900 in Naxxar, Malta
  D/o: Lorenzo & Maria Vittoria Falzon
- **Giuseppa Gauci**
  Born: 02 August 1909 in Naxxar, Malta
  Died: 06 January 2003 in Michigan USA
  — **John Xuereb**
  Born: 06 August 1910 in Mosta, Malta
  Married: 03 November 1929 in St Paul's Bay, Malta
- **Nazzarena Xuereb**
  Born: 09 June 1947 in St Paul's Bay, Malta

Ref. No: 120349 - FTW   D/o = daughter of

LANFRANCO GENEALOGY SERVICES — DAVID LANFRANCO, GENEALOGIST, MALTA

DOLORES

As I previously mentioned, Mother thought for sure we were headed into some God-forsaken pagan land. So much so that she insisted her daughter Maria Dolores (she changed her name to Dolores when she became a U.S. citizen), who was six at the time, make her Confirmation before we left. The date of the Confirmation was the 10th of June 1951, just days before we left for the U.S.A. It was celebrated at the Church of Our Lady of Porto Salvo (San Filippu) in Senglea. The minister was H.L. Mgr. Emmanuele Galea and Dolores' sponsor was Carmela Vassallo, who lived up the road from us. She was a good friend of Mother's. No church on the main island was offering this sacrament before our departure. Mother then arranged to take Dolores to Valletta, Malta's Capitol. There, along with her sponsor, they would catch a ferry to Senglea, where she was given the sacraments of Confirmation.

Note: In Malta, there is a total of 313 churches. In Gozo, there is a total of 46 churches. In all, there are 359 churches on our small islands.

JOSEPHINE GAUCI

My mother was born in the farming village of Naxxar, Malta. She was the second youngest of five children: Vittorja (born in 1903, died on March 18, 1939), Lorenzo (Lawrence) whom they called Wensu (born May 9, 1905, died in 1985 in Australia, where he lived), Marija (born January 23, 1907, died August 30, 1991), Giuseppa (my mom) (born August 2, 1909, died January 6, 2003), and Salvatore (Sam) (born April 19, 1912, died August 21, 2000). Their father Grazio Gauci (born April 29, 1872, died August 21, 1922), was born in another farming village, Gharghur, which is situated next to Naxxar. He was the son of Vincenzo Gauci of Gharghur, and Maria Sciberras of Naxxar. Unfortunately, I never knew our grandparents, neither my mother's nor father's parents, who all hail from the Island of Malta. All four were deceased years before I was even born. Years before my sister Dolores and brother Frank were born. My brother Victor was a mere baby of four months old when the last of our grandparents, Francesca Borg Gauci, died in 1940. I envy people who can remember their grandparents and have fond memories of them. Even worse, we don't even have pictures of three of the four grandparents that I can sit and hold and make any kind of comparisons or similarities. Perhaps this is also a driving factor as to why I am taking the time and effort to write my mother's stories. All I heard was that my Nannu Grazio was a wise farmer and a man with manners. He also worked in the salt pans of Malta in or near St. Paul's Bay in the Salina Bay area. Occasionally, he went fishing for octopus, where my mother, as a child, would remember accompanying him. She would tell stories of the waters turning blue after a catch from the octopus' ink. Their mother was Francesca Borg Gauci, who was married to Grazio on November 11, 1900. A stern and business-like woman, she unfortunately became a young widow on August 21, 1922, when Nannu died in the hospital at Floriana, Malta, of chronic empyema, complications of pneumonia. My mother was only 13 when she lost her father.

Malta lies in the central Mediterranean Sea, 58 miles south of Sicily and 180 miles from the nearest point of the North African mainland. There are three main islands: Malta, Gozo to the northwest, and Comino between them. Malta is 94.9 sq. miles, Gozo is 25.9 sq. miles, and Comino is 2.5 sq. miles. The total coastline is 15.7 miles.

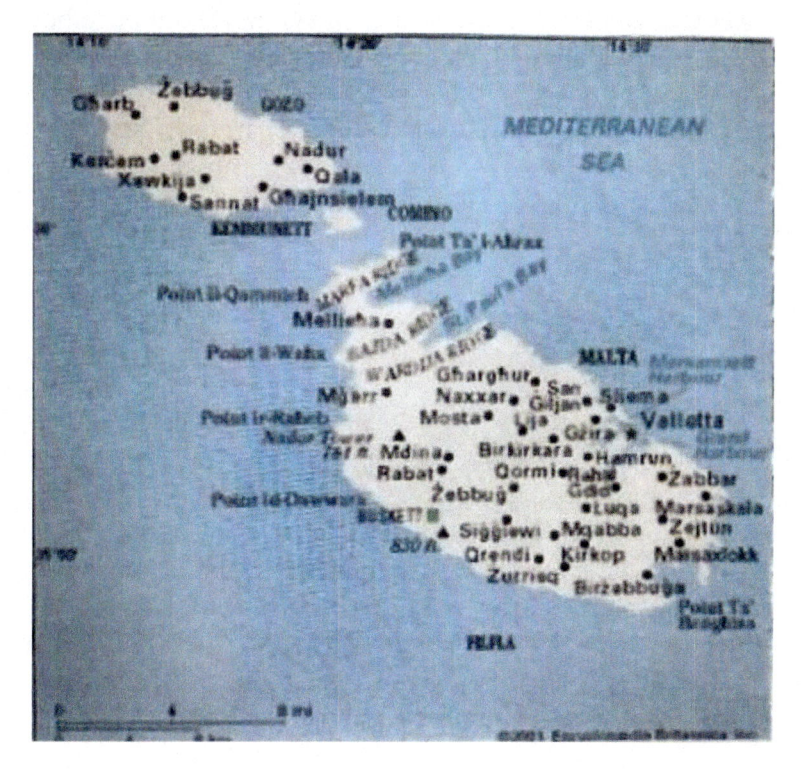

Map of Malta. Notice the proximity of Gharghur, Naxxar and Mosta.

YOUNG JOSEPHINE

One story often told by my mother was the time during dinner when her father Grazio Gauci, would insist on proper table manners: the proper way to hold and use a soup spoon, never having elbows on the table, sitting up straight, etc. One of the earliest incidents Mother recalls was the time she and her sister Marija, just two years older, were arguing at the dinner table about their food. Potatoes were the main daily source of their diet, and meat was a rare commodity, a very scarce luxury, and rarely heard of. When they did have the opportunity for a small amount of meat, my mother and her sister would sit and compare pieces and end up fighting over the size of the cube of meat in their soup bowl. Nannu told my mother to share if she didn't want any more, and my mother, who was very young at the time, selfishly muttered back to my Nannu that she would save it for later as if it were a piece of candy. My Nannu found her comment very humorous considering my mother's young age.

Nannu Grazio Gauci worked in the salt pans near St Paul's Bay and Salina Bay area.

Since they did not have ovens to cook their baked dishes, such as Imqarrun fil-forn (baked macaroni), they would take it to the local baker, generally on Sundays, who would bake these dishes for the villagers in their bread ovens.

Customary cooking pots were used back in the day, and on the floor is a traditional two-tone woven basket called a qoffa, which comes in all shapes and sizes.

WORLD WAR I

As a child, my mother recalls her grandfather living with them. Nannu Vincenzo, her father's dad, was the one young Josephine would call Censu (Vincent) rather than Nannu; why, we're not sure, perhaps she liked the sound of that name, perhaps she heard everyone else call him that as well. She can remember him sitting in a corner and laughing while he made a mess of everything, literally everything from food to bodily waste. She recalls how hard it was for her mother to care for him. Truly, this sounds like another case of dementia or Alzheimer's, but back then, there was so little known about the illness, and everyone merely referred to it as a part of aging. My mother clearly remembers that, since they had an elderly person living with them during World War I, they were entitled to receive a bag of government-issued brown sugar every month or so, and it was my mother's job to go fetch this bag of brown sweetness. Well, she recalls walking home and nibbling on this bag of sugar, which tasted like candy to my mother, who was probably around six years of age. Nevertheless, when she arrived home, it was apparent that some of this brown sugar was missing from the bag, and she feared what would happen, but to her surprise, her mother merely smiled and shook her head. She was so young, but this incident left a lasting embedded memory in her brain.

✠✠✠✠✠

Note: While I'm talking about great Nannu Vincenzo, I have to add a story my mother shared with me. In his younger days, my great Nannu and the men would sit and gather outside, relaxing and talking, just as the men still do today. One fellow asked my great Nannu why he doesn't have a child yet. My great Nannu Vincenzo Gauci quickly replied, "I can't afford any." The men all started to laugh. My great Nannu got a quick lesson in the birds and the bees. You see, the word for having a baby in Maltese is "Tixtri" or "buy." One way of saying this would be, "Ara. Dik il-mara se tixtri!" "Look, that lady is going to have (buy) a baby." After detailed instructions, my great Nannu got the hang of it and quickly multiplied.

✠✠✠✠✠

During another time in Josephine's childhood, she recalls her mother having a different reaction than the brown sugar incident. She said that after Sunday Mass, the ladies would stand around and talk in the church square. Young Josephine saw a very pregnant woman, and out of the blue, without thinking, she pointed and blurted out, "Dik il-mara se tixtri tarbija!" "That lady is going to have a baby!" Before my mother had time to think about what she had just said, a hand came flying across her face. I guess thinking and speaking out loud about that private subject and condition was a complete no.

JOSEPHINE'S YOUNGER YEARS

My mother once shared a story that was very embarrassing to her. Josephine was eight or nine years old during World War I, and her sister was around eleven. They were working on their farm in Qawra when a couple of soldiers casually made their way onto their private fields. These soldiers, seemingly without a care in the world, laughed and tore off grapes from their vines. One soldier walked over to my mother and her sister, who both stood frozen in fear. While one soldier proceeded to touch and stroke her sister's hair, the other instructed my mother to go get them something to drink. Terrified, Josephine ran to her mom as fast as her legs could take her and announced with fear and breathlessness that there were two soldiers by her sister, demanding something to drink. Her mother told her to leave them alone, assuring her they would be gone soon. Mother recounted that as quickly as they came, they were gone, leaving her and her sister shaken.

✠✠✠✠✠

Note: November 11, 2018, marked the 100th anniversary of the end of the Great War – World War 1 (1914-18), which had been described as "the war to end all wars."

MALTESE BAGPIPES

My mother loved the bagpipes. I thought perhaps she heard the Scottish bagpipes at some point in her life and fell in love. I found out that there were bagpipes in Malta as well, called the Zaqq (the stomach). These Maltese bagpipes use bags made out of animal skin, but what makes the Zaqq unique is the form of the bag; it consists entirely of animal skin, complete with legs and a tail, but missing the head. When held horizontally under the arm, upside down, with the legs sticking up, the Zaqq presents an amazing sight. In the past, goats, still-born calves, dogs, and even large cats were used for bags. The younger generation was much too embarrassed by the look and stated it was a thing of the past.

Toni Cachia (I -Hammarun) of Naxxar is the last of the Zagg makers and players of the Zagg. Pictured is Toni playing his calf-skin Zagg in 1972. Note the rubber tubing used as a blowpipe and the way it is held almost horizontally.

MOTHER'S SCHOOLING

Josephine loved school and the entire learning process. She would always tell me how her class was just starting to learn Italian; even later in life, she would sound off her numbers in Italian just to impress us, how she loved to learn! Who knows, if she had lived in a different time, perhaps she would have been able to continue and fulfill her love of knowledge. Unfortunately, that love was cut short when she was in standard 2, equivalent to our American second grade.

She would often go to school with an enormous patch on the back of her dress, and her classmates kept teasing her about it. Kids can be so cruel and mean. She finally complained to her mother that kids were mean to her when she wore her dress with a patch. Her mother simply replied in a harsh, loud voice that SHE COULD QUIT IF SHE WANTED TO. The fact was she didn't want to quit; she loved school and learning, but she didn't want to be taunted by her classmates for wearing a dress with a patch anymore either. She decided never to go back to school, a decision she would regret for years.

One thing she wouldn't miss at school was the sight of bulldozers and pitchforks digging up the graves from the public plots at a cemetery near her school. She could see soil and bones on the forks of this heavy machinery. Soil and bones being lifted from their graves, what a sight for anyone to witness, let alone a small child. Being that private graves weren't much of an option on this small Island of Malta back in the day, Mother explained that the graves were dug up every few years or so and placed in a common area. This left a lasting impression on her young mind, and I'm sure the sight of those human bones was nothing to forget quickly, a vision that stuck with her for life.

Josephine loved math. She could go through her times table like they were nothing. She would do math problems on any piece of paper in her reach. She wrote on anything and everything. I found her math scribbles everywhere, particularly on corners of newspapers, on scrap pieces of paper, and also on envelopes with important documents. She just loved math that much.

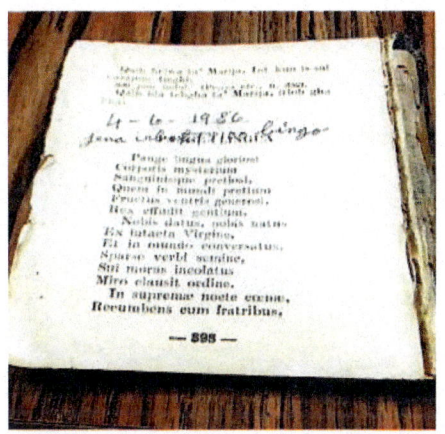

Even in her prayer book, she wrote: (4-6-1986, jiena irbaħt $100.00 bingo) 4-6-1986 I won $100.00 bingo. Perhaps she was thanking God for her winnings.

She also loved to keep track of dates on some of her favorite personal and household items; like her Prell shampoo bottle, Tide laundry detergent, Joy dish soap, Adorn hairspray, etc. She would indicate the date she purchased these items just to see how long they would last. It was a curiosity thing for her, a mere game. I must add that she was loyal to her brand-name products; she never swayed away from a product she liked, even if there were other products on sale.

✠✠✠✠✠

Mother would get so excited when it was that time of the year to get our school supplies; if she could have gone to school with us, she would have. She especially loved the black spotted thin composition notepads that would always have the multiplication times table on the back page of the notepad, how she loved those! She would sit and go over them one at a time and then even mix them up and go through them again. My sister Grace and my brother Joe went to night school for a while when we arrived in Detroit. I know my mother wanted to join them, but everyone laughed and told her there was no need for her to go to school. My other siblings, who were of school age, attended Ste. Anne's School, which was close to the Ambassador Bridge, near our home in Detroit. The same is true for driving; she wanted to learn to drive in the U.S., especially since she learned the basics in Malta on that Jeep my dad owned for a short period. The Jeep story will be explained later.

FARMER'S HYGIENE

Mother would embarrassingly talk about their hygiene as young female farmers. She said it was a weekly ritual to comb their hair with kerosene to remove tangles but also to kill any lice; she talked about how it would burn their scalp. Back then, they used a harsh bar of soap that was cut into several little pieces called "Tac-cavetta" to wash your clothes and also to wash your face, neck, hands up to your elbows and knees down to the feet, but as to your private parts, that was not frequently washed until the winter weather broke, and they could go to the sea for a full-body wash. Mind you, their swim wasn't for recreation as we know it today. My cousin's daughter, Nathalie Caruana, described it as a type of freedom from "dirt." Mother recalls layers of winter grime stuck to her body. She recalls the hardest time was during a girl's menstrual cycle. Since the girls on the farm knew nothing of feminine pads, rags, or hygiene, they literally would go without, unlike the city girls who used torn rags. She couldn't wait to jump into the sea when the weather permitted. Of course, Mother's version was much more descriptive and worded in a way that wasn't so kind on the ears and quite gory to say the least. This was to explain to us how hard it was for a woman in that era to work hard from morning to night on the farm. This taught us values since so many in this day and age take simple things like pads and various other conveniences for granted.

✠✠✠✠✠

Also note that an indoor bathroom was not mandatory in Malta until 1965, give or take a year. I know this because my Zija (aunt) Marija (mother's sister) was just getting a toilet installed during my first return trip to Malta with my mother. (This made me think of the first time Mother had an indoor bathroom; this was when she was 42 years of age when she came to the States.)

Since my mother was unfamiliar with sanitary napkins, as I just mentioned, I have to jump ahead and tell you about when free samples of fragrant panty liners came in the mail when we lived on Baker Street in Detroit, Michigan. During a regular visit, I noticed some objects, maybe four, on the wall of the long hallway in the dining room. When I got a closer look, I belted out, "Mother, what are these doing on the wall?" She said they are air fresheners and they just came in the mail today. When I caught my breath, I told her, "No, they are panty liners." She was so shocked when I explained what they were used for that she immediately ripped them off the wall in haste, hoping no one would come in at that precise moment. After we composed ourselves, we started to laugh, and she said, "How was I supposed to know?"

✠✠✠✠✠

(Although cringeworthy, I added these stories to explain how hard it was for men and women in that era to practice hygiene as it was unknown to them. I wanted to put into perspective that men and women on the farm worked hard in the sweltering heat from morning till night without the modern hygiene that we all know today. Since we all live in a modern age where soap, sanitary napkins, washcloths, and clean running water are easily accessible, I wanted to show the value of the simple conveniences that we often take for granted.)

Gail, Frank, Dad and Manuel.

Ginger, Grace, Mother and Dad.

THE MALTESE STAMINA/FALDETTA AND/OR GĦONNELLA/ĊULQANA

Mother often talked about her stamina. It was also known as a faldetta, għonnella, or ċulqana in other parts of Malta. For clarity, I will describe it as stamina since that is how my mother always referred to it and the term used in her village of Naxxar. I never heard her call it anything else. The stamina covered the head and wrapped around the body from the knee area upward; it did not cover the face. According to the local legend, stamina was first introduced to Malta in 1224 by the women of Celano in the Abruzzi region of Italy as a sign of mourning. Supposedly, they were expelled on the orders of Holy Roman Emperor Frederick II following the massacre of their husbands. For centuries, stamina was worn by virtually all adult Maltese women. It was so popular that there were many seamstresses whose only job was to design, cut, and sew knee-length stamina. Its popularity rapidly fell, however, in the 1940s and 1950s following World War II. I clearly remember seeing them worn in abundance around villages and in churches during my first return visit to Malta with my mother back in 1965. She would go on about her fondness for this piece of garment, how comfortable and convenient it was, this outerwear that accompanied mother everywhere during the course of a day, month, and even years. Mother loved her

One of Mother's prized dolls.

stamina. She loved how it grew with her through pregnancies and how convenient it was while nursing a child. By the 1970s, it was rarely seen at all, except among the older members of the Maltese lay missionary movement, the Societas Doctrinae Christianae, known as (M.U.S.E.U.M.). By the end of the 20th century, it has disappeared altogether. I learned on one of my visits to Malta that the brim was often kept stiff with a whalebone. The Maltese stamina is now seen only in vintage postcards or museums. Collector-type dolls dressed in this traditional outfit are also produced for tourists or memory-seeking Maltese. Mother always picked up one or two of these dolls when in Malta to remind her of days gone by. She enjoyed telling whoever would lend an ear stories of her wearing a stamina. She would hold the doll while touching and stroking the silk fabric and just reminisce.

FRANCESCA BORG GAUCI

(OUR NANNA)

After my Nannu Grazio Gauci passed away from empyema pneumonia in 1922 at the young age of 50, the family of five children -- Vittorja, Wensu (Lawrence), Marija, Josephine, and Salvatore (Sam) -- and the farm were left to be managed by my nanna Francesca. There was no public assistance; you worked hard to survive, and they did. Nanna Francesca was a tough lady, but so was the art of survival and the necessity for life. Nanna Francesca was a shrewd businesswoman who always negotiated the purchase and sale of properties.

My mother and her siblings worked the farm in Qawra. Mother recalls her sister Vittorja always having to stop and rest, and my mother knew there was something seriously wrong with her. In 1939, Vittorja died at the young age of 36 from chronic nephritis, which affects the kidneys and causes severe fatigue. Going to the doctor routinely wasn't heard of, and certainly not for farmers who were struggling to survive. Vittorja never married, although it says "single" and "housewife" on her death certificate; I found that somewhat strange. I noticed it says on a farm in Qawra, address unknown, how sad that an address could not be listed.

My mother also recalled times she and her sister Marija were hired out and had to go and collect horse manure off the streets. She spoke of a time she observed kids swimming in the sea while she and her sister were collecting horse manure. She thought nothing of it until the children started to make fun of mother and her sister while they laughed as they played in the water. She so envied those children and wished they could take a dip in the sea like the other children. They loved the water and felt it was so unfair. While living and farming in Qawra, my mother, and her sister would often sneak out for a quick dip in the afternoon when they were supposed to be napping. When they did nap, Mother recalls going to sleep in the shade and waking up to the full afternoon sun on her face.

Mother's older brother (Lorenzo) Wensu, just 19, left for Adelaide, Australia, on the ship called "Villa De Metz" when mother was 15, just two years after their father's death, arriving in Australia on the 29th of September 1924.

Gauci Family (standing): Mother Josephine and Salvu (seated): Vittorja, Nanna Francesca and Marija.

Post card Picture of Lorenzo, (Wenzu) Gauci from Adelaide, Australia

Mother would often write letters to her brother Wensu for her mom. She did receive a postcard from him many years later, but other than that, she never heard anything of him or about him after he departed from Malta until shortly after his death years later.

My mom received news of her brother Wensu's death during a trip to Malta. It pained her that she didn't hear sooner, but I think he had just died. The parish priest of Naxxar was notified of his death and took care of any last will. We don't believe Ziju Wensu had a family in Australia. Salvu also moved to Australia later in 1949 with his wife Grazia and seven children.

Nanna Francesca.

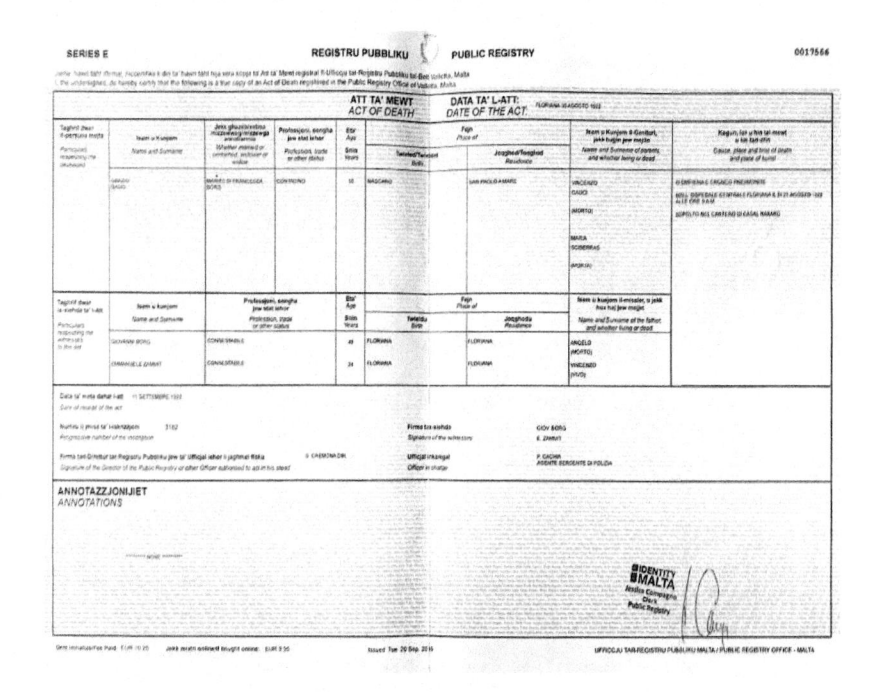

Death certificate of Nannu Grazio Gauci (our Nannu).

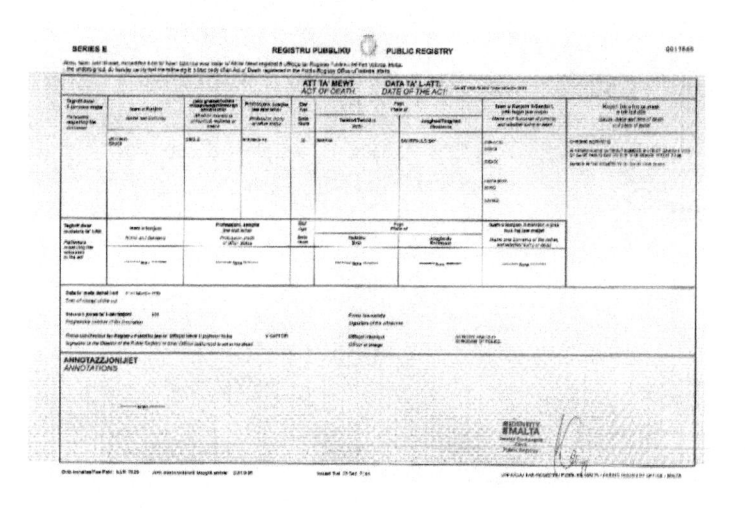

Zija Victoria Gauci's death certificate (Mother's sister).

Nanna Francesca Gauci farming in Qawra.

The front of the Qawra farm.

Other buildings on the farm which is located across from today's Kennedy Grove.

Ziju Lorenzo's passport application.

Once in Australia, Salvu started a fruit and vegetable stand that has grown into a large grocery store, Minchinbury Fruit Market, in New South Wales, Australia, which is still run by the family.

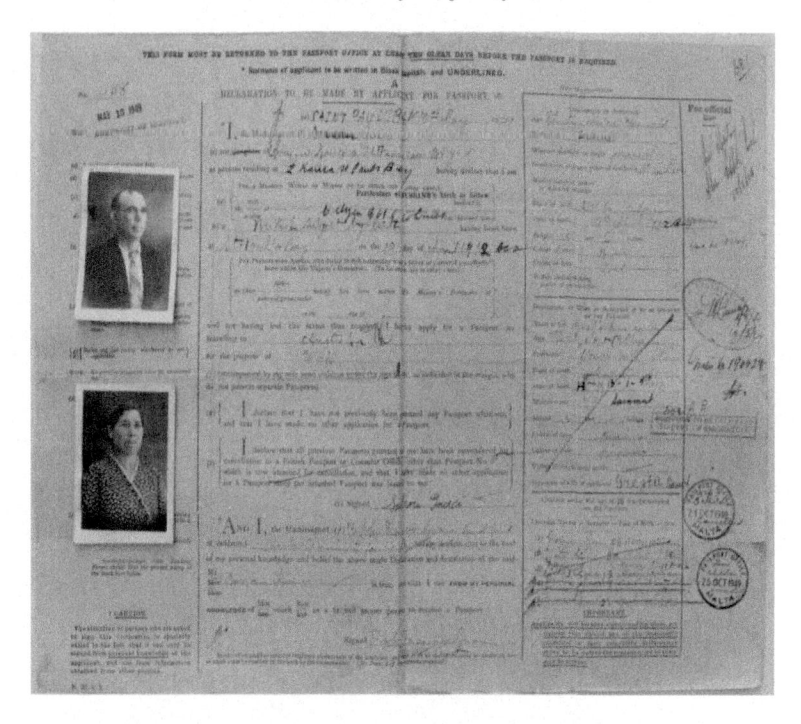

Ziju Salvu and his wife Grazia Zammut Gauci's passport application.

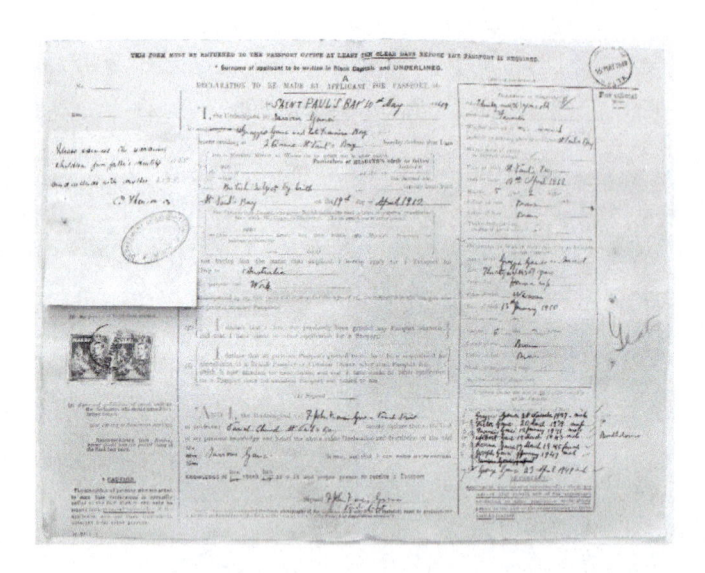

The Gauci children's portion of the passport application names seven children in the lower right. Note that the youngest was born just a month before the application, and another son was born in Australia.

Ziju Salvu Gauci with his wife Grazia Sammut Gauci with their seven sons and one daughter. This family photo was taken in Australia.

THE MARRIAGE

I'm told and have read that in Malta, when a girl becomes of age and the family is ready to find a husband for their daughter, a pot of flowers or sweets is set outside the window indicating to any potential suitor that a girl is ready for courtship. Mother often told us about the time this took place in their household, but there was a small problem.

Under traditional circumstances, my dad would have found an older man who could act as a "huttab" (marriage broker). This huttab would have notified my nanna Francesca of my dad's interest, and if they agreed, a contract would have been drawn up, and the dowry would have been put in place.

When my father inquired, it was my Zija Marija who was being offered her hand in marriage. He paid the broker his customary fee of £1 (one Maltese lira) (approximately $3.00) and told him he would handle this himself and bypass all the formality.

Dad went to explain to my nanna Francesca that it was Josephine he fancied and wanted. She was two years younger than her sister, and my father was a year younger than Josephine. He said there was too much of an age difference between him and Marija.

My Dad went on to explain that his mother, Marianna, always told him that if he married an older woman, she would die before him, and he would have to bring up the children alone. Nanna Francesca gave it a lot of thought and allowed my dad to take my mom's hand in marriage. Once agreed, a dowry was in place, and a marriage was finally in motion after a short wait.

My mother had no say in the matter. She remembered the eve of the wedding, sitting on the rooftop, swinging her legs in amazement, and telling herself that she was getting married the next day. Here she was, 20 years of age, getting married, like it or not, and knowing so little of the man she was about to spend the rest of her life with, the man who eventually would tear her away from her birthplace to a new world.

She recalls on November 3, 1929, the day of the wedding, seeing my dad in the church at Our Lady of Sorrow in St. Paul's Bay and barely recognizing him all cleaned up and in a suit. During the wedding reception, mother recalls sitting on a chair and forming a large pocket on her lap with her black wedding skirt while guests tossed or dropped gold rings and trinkets as gifts. Her mother suggested, rather insisted, that she share some rings with her two sisters. My Zija Marija eventually married, nine years later, Gamri Gauci, her first cousin, who was 15 years older. This practice wasn't unusual.

Note: Dad's older sister Vittorja knew Mother's mom, Francesca Borg Gauci, as they were friends before the marriage. Dad's mother, Marianna died just ten months before the wedding.

Giuseppa Gauci (20) and Giovanni Xuereb (19) marriage November 3, 1929 at the Church of Our Lady of Sorrows, St. Paul's Bay.

Photos of Mother and Dad.

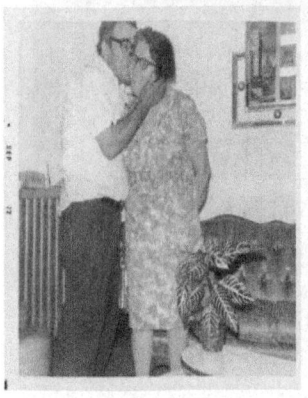

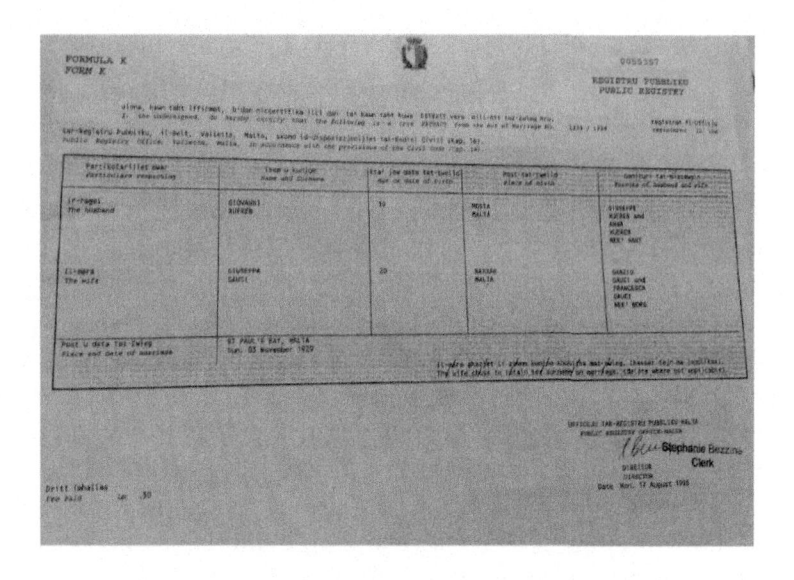

John Xuereb & Josephine Gauci's marriage certificate.

Church of Our Lady of Sorrows, St. Paul's Bay, where John & Josephine were married.

FEAST OF ST. PETER/ST. PAUL

Part of a marriage dowry back then was a promise that during the first year of marriage, the husband was expected to take his bride to a couple of major feasts. One is the L-Imnarja on the 29th of June. A national feast since the rule of the Knights, L-Imnarja is a traditional Maltese festival of food, religion, music, and, of course, horse racing, which has been popular since 1722. The festivities are still being held today. This feast commemorates the martyrdoms of St. Peter and St. Paul. On the eve of this feast day, many people gather at Buskett Gardens, a small forested area outside Rabat, to eat rabbit stew and drink local wine, as well as to listen to folk singing, known as l-għana. The traditional singing l-għana is a simple and spontaneous song of the Maltese peasantry sung by the people of the village. The l-għana are melancholic, something between a Sicilian ballad and the rhythmic wail of an Arabic tune that seems to express the sadness of centuries-old tales of impassionate love. I rather like that description, but simply put, two peasants often carry-on spontaneous conversation in rhyming high pitch, chanting back and forth with speed and ease, producing laughter from the crowds, evidence of native skill and humor. The singers are accompanied by a guitarist. The festivities last until the early hours of the morning.

Church of Our Lady of Sorrows where Mother and Dad were married and Frank and Rena were baptized.

LIFE ON THE FARM

Mother took up with her new husband and lived on her mom's farm in the beginning, as customary, then immediately went from her mother's farm and moved to her husband's shared farm in Ghajn Rihana. This farm has been worked for years by two brothers, Paul and Anne Gauci, and Salvu and Carmela Gauci, and their cousins, my dad, John, and Josephine Xuereb. Living and sharing the space in a 100-year lease owned by the church. A fee of £1 (one Maltese lira) was paid in rent per year, approximately $3.00. The upstairs part of the farm was occupied by my dad's cousin Salvu Gauci, and his wife, Carmen Vassallo Gauci. I remember Mother saying that this poor woman had lost a baby because of a miscarriage and cried and cried for months until she fell pregnant again and then ended up having three boys. Another cousin was Paul Gauci; he shared a few of the rooms with his wife, Anne Vassallo Gauci, and their family of five children. Anne and Carmen were sisters. A son, Joe, and daughter, Rose, still farm the land today. Their dad did build a beautiful house right next to the homestead some years back.

Mother loved that farm; no rugs or wood floors but rather rough poured cement floors. It was her castle. She loved the whole farming life, the crops, the chickens, pigs, sheep, cattle, and, of course, the famous horse and cow, which I will tell you more about later. My dad had a hog breeding business with a sign posted outside and all. This pig must have been quite a stud, as he was pretty busy. His .50 cent services even came with a guarantee.

Life on the farm was hard, never-ending work. The family worked the farm barefooted, and the bottom of their feet looked like shoe leather, thick and hard. While working the land, my older sister Grace stepped on broken glass that Dad later drenched kerosene all over. She inherited a souvenir of the hard life on the farm. Something she would show her children years later. I remember going on walks with Grace while she walked the sheep. I had a small dwarf lamb that I tended to.

✠✠✠✠✠

Dad later bought an old farmhouse that was just down the street and around the corner from us. He bought it "bil Chance," which means the seller had a six-month chance to take the property back. My dad made the mistake of starting to work on the property immediately. The seller decided to take the property back. My dad was upset, but I understand the seller paid my dad for the materials used. Today, it is a beautiful piece of property with a swimming pool.

✠✠✠✠✠

On August 24, 1930, just nine months and three weeks after my parent's wedding, my sister Marija Assunta was born. It was customary to name the children after the grandparents out of respect. She was born in a flat just down the street from the famous Mosta Rotunda Church. It wasn't unusual to keep a flat for special occasions such as births, parties, baptism, communion, and such. This flat saw the births of five others, not including Frank nor myself. I will explain why as I write more. Our flat on Hope Street is now one of several lottery offices near the Rotunda.

Sixteen months later, on December 10, 1931, my sister Grazia was born, also at the Mosta flat. Now you can imagine, with two daughters and no son, all the teasing my father had to endure from his friends. Mother felt bad, but she loved having two beautiful baby girls. She found herself sewing dresses on a hand-cranked sewing machine that once belonged to her older sister Vittorja. She loved pampering her daughters. She truly enjoyed that time in her life.

Flat in Mosta on Hope Street, just down the street from the Mosta Rotunda.

Mother remembers that sewing machine being purchased at the Naxxar Trade Fair, a fair that was in town for about two weeks each year. This was the place where the people on the island could view all the latest appliances and ware out on the market. Mother brought this sewing machine with her to the States. She enjoyed crocheting different symbols like crosses, chalices, etc. When she was done crocheting, she would sew her work onto the best Irish linen she could find, then donate them to various churches for their altars.

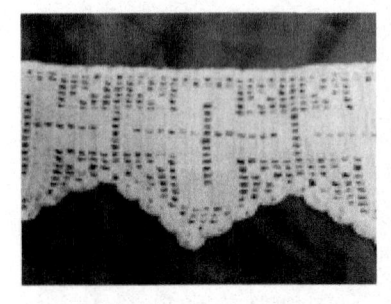

Almost four and a half years after the birth of Grace, and I'm sure a few miscarriages in between, my brother Giuseppe was born on April 23, 1936. My mother was excited to bear a son for my dad and told him he no longer had to deal with all the teasing from his friends. My father immediately told Mother that never bothered him since he loved his girls. Joe, being the first-born son, was a constant companion for my dad.

After Joe, there were two more boys, but not until a little girl named Vittorja was taken on March 19, 1939, just 14 hours old. Every year on St. Joseph's Day, March 19th, Mother was very quiet and spent the day thinking of her newborn that was taken much too soon. Her story she told me was that this tiny baby girl named Vittorja had a lot of phlegm and trouble breathing at birth. Mother was told by the midwife to keep the baby on her side. In Malta, a child is generally baptized the next day, and the party is held shortly after. Mother recalls her mom coming over with a friend to the party to see the baby who was crying in her crib. This lady decided to pick up the baby even after my mother asked her not to. The lady pulled my sister and her blanket up and held her close while swaying back and forth in a rocking motion. The baby soon stopped crying and was put back in her crib with her blanket still covering her face. Mother instinctively went to check on her baby, but the lady said she was ok; she was sleeping. Shortly after, my father went over to show off his bundle of joy to a visitor and found her not breathing and already blue. My father was devastated. My mother blamed herself for listening to this lady rather than checking on her infant daughter, as her mother's instinct told her. She died just 14 hours after birth from Pulmonary Atelectasis, which is a complete or partial collapse of the entire lung. It occurs when the tiny air sacs within the lung become deflated possibly filled with fluid.

Shortly after my brother Vittorio was born on June 8, 1940, in the Mosta flat, as were the ones before him, only this time was the start of World War II. I couldn't imagine taking cover in an air raid shelter with small children, let alone a baby. The first bombing attack by the Italians was on the 11th of June 1940. A point of fact: Victor was actually born on May 31st, and all these years, we celebrated on the 8th of June. On one of my Malta visits, Victor asked me to pick up his birth certificate. I gave the clerk the information, and he couldn't find anything but said he found one for May 31st. I said that's impossible he was born in June. He said all the information matched his parents and his farm address.

On August 10, 1942, Frangisk was born, only this time, my mother never made it to the Mosta flat due to the war. Frank was born on the farm, in the upper bedroom located at 82 Burmarrad Road, in Ghajn Rihana, which was within the St. Paul's Bay boundaries at the time.

Marija Dolores was born two-and-a-half years after Frank on January 25, 1945. Mother did indeed make it to the birthing/party flat in Mosta on Hope Street this time. My father described Dolores as an angel with a fair complexion and green eyes. My brothers Joe and Frank also had green eyes, whereas my oldest sister Marija and dad had blue eyes. The rest of us were born with brown eyes like my mom.

Lastly, I, Nazarena came into this world on June 9th of 1947, and I did not make it to the Mosta flat on Hope Street. I don't exactly know why, maybe after giving birth seven plus times, Mom just wanted to stay on the farm she loved.

Yes, I too, along with Frank and years later nephew Jimmy Gatt, were born in the upper room with that beautifully decorated brick with the Rod of Asclepius carved onto it.

The Rod of Asclepius outside the birthing room.

The birthing room on the farm.

The symbol of many medical associations: a rod with a serpent wrapped around it. Perhaps once the farmhouse of a physician. Each time I ride the bus when in Malta, I point out that window to every stranger who will take a look. I announce that is where I was born. My siblings tell me how they were all told to go play all day at the neighbor's house, the Gatts', whose farm was directly behind ours.

They thought that was pretty unusual, and they wondered why. The siblings, most of whom were still pretty young, came home later in the day to find a new crying baby on the farm, a baby that wasn't there earlier; they got to thinking. Unlike my fair green-eyed sister Dolores, I was born on the darker side with hair everywhere. Mother, bless her heart, immediately thought what a blessing; she will never marry, she will be with me forever.

Frank on the farm in 1974 looking at the well he once fell in as a child.

Dolores pictured with Joe and Rose Gauci who still lived at and tended to the farm, 1974.

Views of the farm at Ghajn Rihana in 1978, photos courtesy of Rod Xuereb.

Sewing machine which was brought to America.

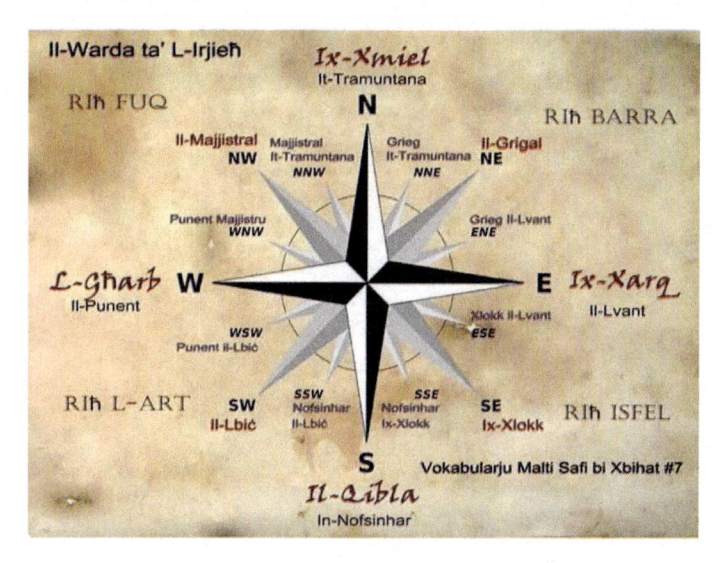

As a farmer, mother often spoke of the wind direction shown on this chart.

73

> **Għajn Rehana, limits of**
>
> Borg Josephine — —
> Camilleri Anna — Farmhouse
> Camilleri Pacifica — —
> Chetcuti Ganna — —
> Chetcuti Ignatius, Ta' Sarima — —
> Galea Carmelo — Farmhouse
> Galea Francesco — Farmhouse
> Gatt Maria — —
> Gatt Salvu, Tal-Gżejjer — —
> Gauci Karmena — —
> Muscat John, Tal-Ħalib — —
> Sant Carmela — —
> Sant Ignazia — —
> Sant Paul, Ta' Xewwex — —
> Vassallo Bertu, Ta' Mejju — —
> Vassallo Carmela née Camilleri — —
> Vassallo Carmela of Joseph — —
> Vassallo Thomas, Ta' Mejju — —
> Xuereb Giuseppa — 82
> Xuereb John, Ta' Grima

Names of neighbors I heard my mother speak of all my life.

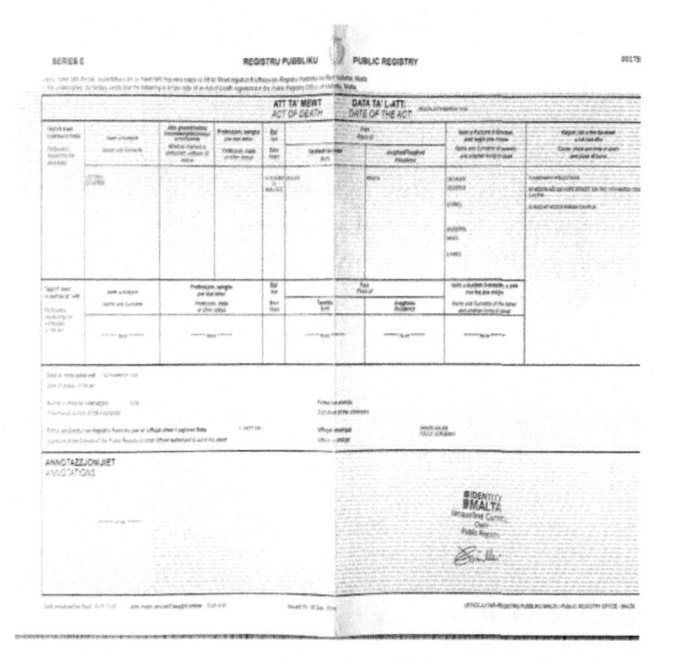

Death Certificate of Vittoria Xuereb at just 14 hours old.

Just to the right of the upper birthing window is the entrance to the farm.

MARIJA'S HERNIA

Mother would often speak of the farming way of life. She was used to it all her life, but now married and with an infant daughter, it seemed even harder. She recalls how she would often wrap Marija, feed her, and go off to work the farm while the baby slept in the hammock. When she returned, Marija would be crying, often heard by the neighbors. This happened several times, and because of this, Marija developed a hernia. Mother felt awful and blamed herself. I don't think she ever forgave herself for that, but what was one to do when there were so many chores to be done around a farm.

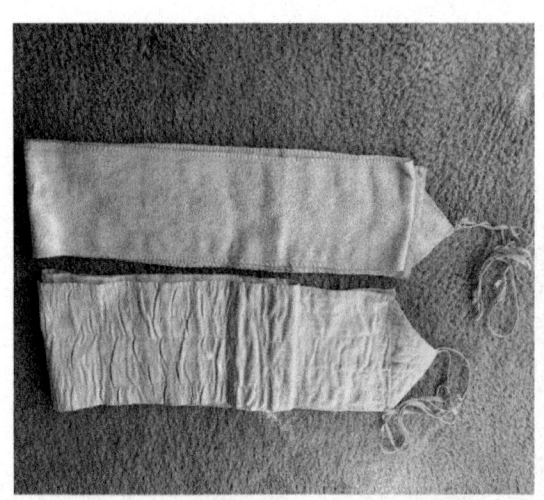

✠✠✠✠✠

Mother would tell me how she would sew long swaddling wraps made of cotton that were three to four inches wide and four to five feet long, with shoelaces sewn to the V-shaped end. Mother would wrap this around the baby's extremities several times and over the homemade diaper, tying it with the shoelace. Not only did she tell me about the swaddling wraps she used for all of us, but she even demonstrated them on my daughter Maria when she was a newborn in 1969. You see, Nanna brought them over with her when we left Malta; they were that important to her, or perhaps she felt she may still need them. They are now among my prized possessions. I pull them out from time to time and just imagine those days, the task it took to change an infant, all the constant wrapping and unwrapping. These strips of cloth were considered a necessity for the baby's first few months. In the olden days, they thought this type of swaddling would help produce better posture in the infant.

DRINKING PETROL

My brother Victor, while quite young, was thirsty and decided to pick up the first jug he saw and drank what turned out to be petrol (gasoline), thinking nothing of it, thinking it was water. This, in turn, made him very ill, obviously, and he had to be taken to see a doctor. Once there, the doctor examined him and asked my mother what he ate or drank. Mother was so embarrassed she quickly replied that she didn't know. This angered the doctor, and he firmly asked her again what did he have to drink, and she said, "Petrol, I think he drank some petrol." The doctor rudely replied, "Well, why didn't you say that in the first place." I firmly believe that because mother was a farmer's wife, the doctor felt he could belittle and talk down to her. I'm sure his tone of voice would have been quite different if she were a mother from the city.

INHERITANCE

    Victor recalls a time as a very young boy, accompanying his dad when he was summoned to a farm for his inheritance. Victor doesn't recall the details of who passed away or, who the inheritance was from, or even what farm they went to, but when they arrived, Dad was told his inheritance was in the other room. He made his entrance to a room containing nothing but a clay pot. Upon setting his eyes on this clay pot, Victor said Dad was filled with rage and immediately kicked the pot and broke it into several small pieces. Victor recalls them leaving the farmhouse without saying a word. We never knew who left Dad that lone clay pot, but Dad wasn't happy with it.

THE THREE BROTHERS

Living on a farm had its ups and downs. My brother Frank recalls walking to school approximately half a mile away with his older brothers Joe and Victor in the rural area near Burmarrad. Since there were no designated sidewalks, the boys had to walk along brush and over several rocks and pebbles while watching every step they took. Frank was terrified of snakes, even though Malta does not have any poisonous ones. He stepped very slowly and carefully during that 10-minute or so walk. Joe, on the other hand, looked for trouble. He would climb trees looking for birds and frogs. Joe had no fear or mercy for these poor creatures, and I can't even describe on paper the fate of those little creatures he managed to catch.

✠✠✠✠✠

As my brothers Victor and Frank often did, they picked fruit from fields to take home or sell. On one particular afternoon, they worked very hard to gather their harvest only to have it stolen by older boys, bullies from the city. Victor laughs at it today, recalling how he and Frank merely turned over the lout without hesitation, saying that was an easy score for the city boys.

RETURNING TO MALTA

I graduated from Holy Redeemer High School in Detroit in 1965. My Dad suggested I take my mother to Malta since it has been 14 years since our departure. We booked through Larry Zahra, our Maltese Consulate who also had a travel agency. Larry arranged many group trips to Malta. People were very appreciative. One could choose from several different lengths of stay.

We took the seven-week trip; after all, we had a lot of catching up to do with my sister, family, and friends. Our plane was full of Maltese, young and old. Our group stopped in England for the day, and I pitied the couple who was responsible for the 200-plus Maltese passengers, young and old. I don't recall what the itinerary was for England or where they stayed, but Mother and I immediately took a cab to Oxford, an hour or so ride to meet my Zija Sr. Carmela Xuereb, who was living there at the time. We had a wonderful visit, spent the night there, and headed back to the airport to meet up with our group. My sister and her husband Joe, along with their six children, greeted us at the airport, and everyone was extremely happy to have their Nanna in Malta. We had a beautiful seven weeks. We spent a lot of time catching up with relatives and friends. Mother realized how Americanized she had become when a group of women surrounded her at the Mosta Church Piazza after mass one day. "Arra Guza, il Americana." "Look, it's Josephine, the American." They admired her dress, heels, and purse; she was a celebrity to them. It made Mother feel good, but that didn't change how she felt; she never wanted to leave her homeland. I was privileged to visit and photograph all but one of my dad's siblings: Angelo, Vittorja (no photo), Salvu, Censu, and Sr. Carmen. Ziju

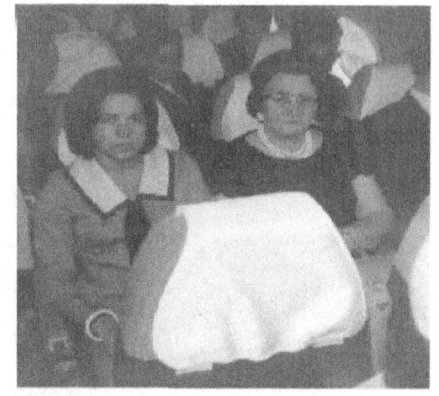

Rena & Mother on the plane to Malta.

Emmanuel lives in Detroit. We also visited my mom's sister, Marija Gauci, since she was the lone sibling who was left in Malta. They reunited during our long stay. Two brothers left for Australia years prior. I don't believe there was any mail exchanged during the 14 years of absence.

✠✠✠✠✠

I took Mother to Malta one Christmas in 1980. Throughout the entire trip, she kept saying, "xi qziez" "What silliness" every time she saw a decorated Christmas tree or wrapped gifts. She would reiterate that Christmas meant going to midnight mass, carrying their shoes, and returning back to the farm.

Marija in the center with all of her siblings: Grace, Joe, Victor, Frank, Dolores, and Rena

Marija wanted all of us to be in Malta for her 50th wedding anniversary.

Cousin Frances in front of the renovated flat.

Mother & Sr. Carmela Xuereb RSCJ in Oxford, England.

Renovations have been made, the alley is beautiful and so green, so inviting.

Marija and Dad at Bugibba.   *Mother and Marija on the beach.*

Dolores and Rena visiting with cousin Frances while in Malta..

MOM AND DAD'S SIBLINGS

Mom's sister in front of the Naxxar flat Cousin Frances, Zija (Aunt) Marija, and Mother.

Speranza Buhagiar Xuereb and Ziju (uncle) Angelo Xuereb.

Mother, Ziju Salvu, daughter Teresa & son Toni Xuereb (not pictured: Dad's sister Vittorja).

Ziju Censu (Vincent), daughter Angela Granddaughter Sr. Mary and grandson Fr. Vince.

Ziju Emmanuel in the middle, my Dad, and finally Zija Sr. Carmela RSCJ.

✠✠✠✠✠

The Xuerebs were part of the 2500-year-old Jewish community in Tunisia on the island of Djerba. The synagogue of El Ghriba is one of the oldest and most beautiful standing synagogues around today. The Xuerebs were not only Jewish but also high priests during their period in Tunisia.

JEWELRY

During our first visit to Malta in 1965, Mother took a large bag of "old" 18K gold and filigree jewelry that she'd had for years back to Malta to be traded. Most likely, jewelry she had as a young bride or purchased before we left Malta. I remember the jeweler in Valletta weighing my mother's bag of gold and replacing it with one common 18K gold, inch-long Maltese cross. That seemed rather odd and unfair to me, but what did I know? Mother never questioned the jeweler, and to this day, I wonder how many other unsuspecting victims he and other jewelers cheated.

✠✠✠✠✠

My husband, Fernando Campos, is a certified gemologist and goldsmith, and when I explained this to him years later, he said that was wrong. That one gold cross couldn't have weighed as much as a bag of gold pieces, some with intricate designs.

LAQAM

Laqam meaning a nickname from the Arabic association meaning "to graft" or "to engrave." On the Maltese Island, this fits perfectly because so many people have the same surname (as shown). Giving them nicknames is the perfect solution. These nicknames stay with the family or individual forever. For example, my dad is Ganni Ta-Grima. I see that back in the 1800s, he had a Nanna with the last name of Grima; perhaps he inherited that name from her. My mother, on the other hand, had a Nanna who made noodles; she was nicknamed Tal-Ghagin. My brother-in-law Joe Gatt was referred to as Tal-Gzejjer. The list goes on; everyone on the island had and has a nickname. The older Maltese come out and ask you what your laqam is as that is how they identify a person. A laqam could be a family name, a business, something comical, something crude, a talent, or almost anything.

The Ranking of Surnames

Borg is leading: 1 in 25 Maltese carry this name. The top 10 surnames represent ¼ of all Maltese surnames.

1. BORG	21. CALLEJA	41. AZZOPARDI	61. BONELLO	81. CILIA	101. PULLICINO
2. VELLA	22. PORTELLI	42. PSAILA	62. FORMOSA	82. CURMI	102. AXISA
3. FARRUGIA	23. GATT	43. VASSALLO	63. CASHA	83. TEUMA	103. GAFA
4. CAMILLERI	24. GRIMA	44. ZAHRA	64. CIANTAR	84. GRISTI	104. BAJADA
5. ZAMMIT	25. BUGEJA	45. SALIBA	65. ZERAFA	85. BALKAN	105. PULIS
6. GRECH	26. MALLIA	46. CACHIA	66. TONNA	86. AZZOPARDI	106. ABDILLA
7. GALEA	27. MIZZI	47. AZZOPARD	67. DALLI	87. DINGLI	107. GRECH/GREG
8. CARUANA	28. BUSUTTIL	48. MAGRO	68. CHETCUTI	88. SAYD	108. FITENI
9. AGIUS	29. SAMMUT	49. MANGION	69. FRENDO	89. CAMENZULI	109. GERADA
10. CASSAR	30. ABELA	50. BARBARA	70. DARMANIN	90. PARNIS	110. CASSIA
11. ATTARD	31. GAUCI	51. MAMO	71. BONAVIA	91. CUMBO	111. RIZZO
12. MICALLEF	32. FALZON	52. BARTOLO	72. TANTI	92. CREMONA	112. CORDINA
13. MIFSUD	33. XERRI	53. BEZZINA	73. CALLUS	93. ABEJER	113. DELIA
14. SPITERI	34. XICLUNIA	54. XUEREB	74. SANT	94. CATANIA	114. CIAPPARA
15. PACE	35. BUTTIGIEG	55. ZARB	75. FELICI	95. CARDONA	115. COLEIRO
16. MUSCAT	36. CAUCHI	56. CUTAJAR	76. DE BRINCAT	96. CUSCHIERI	116. SULTANA
17. BONNICI	37. AQUILINA	57. BUHAGIAR	77. BRIFFA	97. CINI	117. BIGENI
18. FENECH	38. ELLUL	58. DIMECH	78. CHIRCOP	98. GALDES	118. STIVALA
19. SCHEMBRI	39. TABONE	59. MERCIECA	79. PISANO	99. SACCO	119. SOLTANA
20. DEBONO	40. XIBERRAS	60. BALDACCHINO	80. SEICHEL	100. REFALO	120. XIRIHA

MOSTA

In April 1942, when air bombardments were at their worst in Malta, a German bomb fell on the Rotunda during Mass, pierced the dome, fell onto the Church pavement, and bounced against the wall - but failed to explode. A replica of the 440 lbs. bomb is now preserved in the sacristy and exposed to public view. The Rotunda Church and the famous bomb have helped to make Mosta a prosperous little town and a mecca for visitors from all parts of Europe and the world.

The town of Mosta is in the center of the island, which is a busy city and also a market town. The Rotunda is known for its enormous unsupported dome, which is the fourth largest in the world. The Rotunda was constructed between 1833 and 1860 near the site of the old church. The older church, dating back to 1641, was left in place during the construction of the new church. It was only dismantled in 1860 when the Rotunda was almost completed. The church is a circular structure with a cone-shaped dome. No scaffolding was used during construction because its walls are about 20 feet thick. It is very similar to the Pantheon of Rome.

As mentioned, the Rotunda is dedicated to the Assumption of the Virgin Mary, and during the week of August 15th, the town celebrates a joyful celebration, "Il-Festa," with street decorations, music, fireworks, and a religious procession with the statue of Our Lady. The Mosta church has become the ninth church in Malta to be conferred the title of basilica.

Both photos: Mother & Rena on sister Marija's balcony in 1985 enjoying the feast of Santa Marija, which is celebrated on August 15th of each year.

Another important day in Mosta's calendar is Good Friday. This is when the Passion of Christ is re-enacted: men in chains and barefooted, men dressed as soldiers, someone scantily clad portraying Jesus Christ carrying a wooden cross through the streets of Mosta, and children dressed as shepherds line the streets. Several statues are carried through the town in this long, well-orchestrated procession.

FATHER'S PARENTS

Dad never mentioned his parents in conversation, and our mother told us a few brief stories, but other than that, we know absolutely nothing about my father's parents other than what was discovered after some research. We found that they married on September 1, 1895, in Mosta, Malta. His father, Giuseppe (Joseph) Xuereb, was born on June 15, 1866, and his mother, Marianna Sant, was born on March 14, 1872, and died of a cerebral hemorrhage on January 24, 1928. Mother reiterated stories of seeing my father or his brothers taking their mother on a horse and open cart and how she would be sitting with no care in the world and acting like a child. Perhaps this was the onset of dementia that has plagued so many of our family members.

My father was born on August 6, 1910, in the city of Mosta. Like my mother, who was the second youngest in her family of five children, he was also the second youngest, but his family had seven children: Angelo (born August 22, 1896, died October 28, 1971), Salvatore (Sam) (born February 27, 1898, died May 25, 1973), Vittorja (born January 16, 1900, died September 24, 1969), Vincenzo (Vincent) called Censu (born November 23, 1901, died December 24, 1976), Emmanuele (Manuel) (born October 19, 1907, died December 17, 1984), Giovanni (John) my dad was born (born August 6, 1910, died January 18, 1980) and Sr. Carmela (born February 18, 1916, died February 21, 1986). Their aunt Carmela Sant Gauci, Nanna Marianna's sister, took the younger children after Marianna Xuereb's death until after the death of her husband, Michele Gauci. Carmela left Malta for New Orleans, Louisiana, in 1932 to join her son, the priest. Consequently, Carmela had to place my Zija Carmela Xuereb, who was 16, in a convent where she lived her life as a Sister of the Sacred Heart. The boys all managed on their own.

DAD'S GENEALOGY

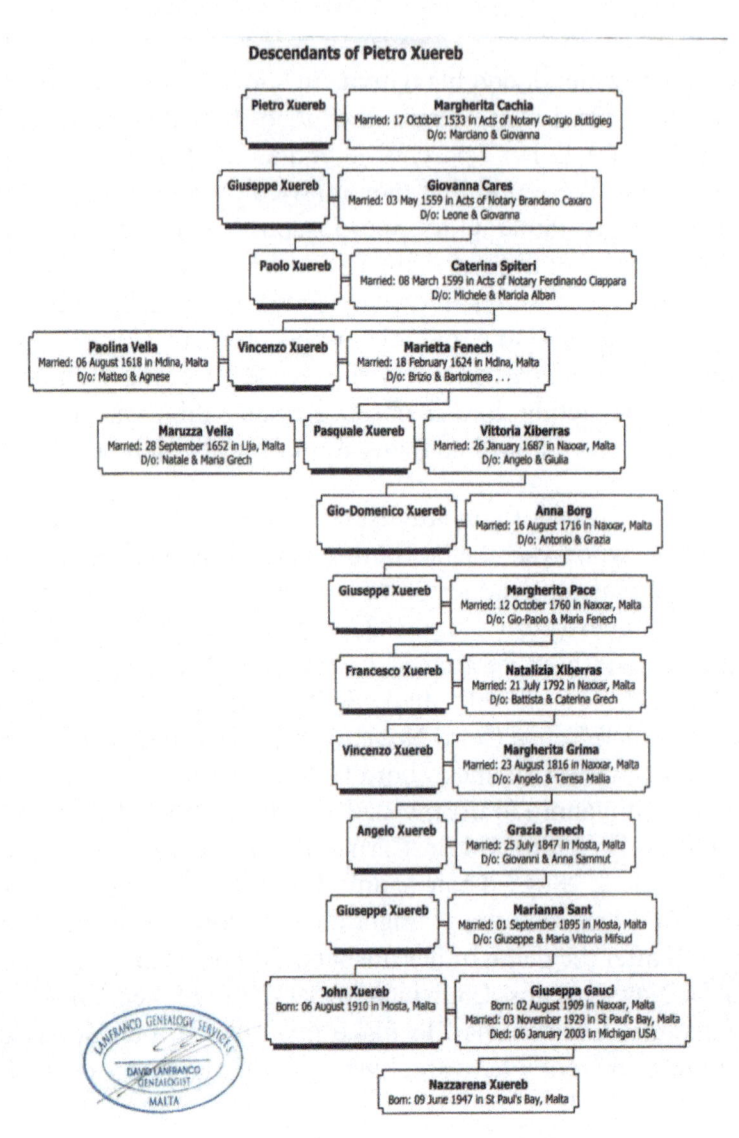

Descendants of Pietro Xuereb

- **Pietro Xuereb**
  - **Margherita Cachia**
    - Married: 17 October 1533 in Acts of Notary Giorgio Buttigieg
    - D/o: Marciano & Giovanna

- **Giuseppe Xuereb**
  - **Giovanna Cares**
    - Married: 03 May 1559 in Acts of Notary Brandano Caxaro
    - D/o: Leone & Giovanna

- **Paolo Xuereb**
  - **Caterina Spiteri**
    - Married: 08 March 1599 in Acts of Notary Ferdinando Ciappara
    - D/o: Michele & Mariola Alban

- **Vincenzo Xuereb**
  - **Paolina Vella**
    - Married: 06 August 1618 in Mdina, Malta
    - D/o: Matteo & Agnese
  - **Marietta Fenech**
    - Married: 18 February 1624 in Mdina, Malta
    - D/o: Brizio & Bartolomea ...

- **Pasquale Xuereb**
  - **Maruzza Vella**
    - Married: 28 September 1652 in Lija, Malta
    - D/o: Natale & Maria Grech
  - **Vittoria Xiberras**
    - Married: 26 January 1687 in Naxxar, Malta
    - D/o: Angelo & Giulia

- **Gio-Domenico Xuereb**
  - **Anna Borg**
    - Married: 16 August 1716 in Naxxar, Malta
    - D/o: Antonio & Grazia

- **Giuseppe Xuereb**
  - **Margherita Pace**
    - Married: 12 October 1760 in Naxxar, Malta
    - D/o: Gio-Paolo & Maria Fenech

- **Francesco Xuereb**
  - **Natalizia Xiberras**
    - Married: 21 July 1792 in Naxxar, Malta
    - D/o: Battista & Caterina Grech

- **Vincenzo Xuereb**
  - **Margherita Grima**
    - Married: 23 August 1816 in Naxxar, Malta
    - D/o: Angelo & Teresa Mallia

- **Angelo Xuereb**
  - **Grazia Fenech**
    - Married: 25 July 1847 in Mosta, Malta
    - D/o: Giovanni & Anna Sammut

- **Giuseppe Xuereb**
  - **Marianna Sant**
    - Married: 01 September 1895 in Mosta, Malta
    - D/o: Giuseppe & Maria Vittoria Mifsud

- **John Xuereb**
  - Born: 06 August 1910 in Mosta, Malta
  - **Giuseppa Gauci**
    - Born: 02 August 1909 in Naxxar, Malta
    - Married: 03 November 1929 in St Paul's Bay, Malta
    - Died: 06 January 2003 in Michigan USA

- **Nazzarena Xuereb**
  - Born: 09 June 1947 in St Paul's Bay, Malta

Ref. No: 120349 - FTW   D/o = daughter of

*Dad with his phony mustache, being funny.
"Xuereb" means man with mustache.*

John Xuereb (Dad).

Dad with his homemade trailer. *Dad.*

Victor and George with their Dad Salvu Gatt, Father of Joe Gatt.

DAD AND SCHOOL

Dad attended no school at all during his youth. He could neither read nor write in any language. Dad managed to start a new life in a foreign country without being able to read or write. How amazing is that? I especially admire him for this. I panic when I go overseas and can't read a sign in another language. My dad went through his whole life this way.

Our Dad would always make his mark with an "X" on anything that needed his signature, but with changing times, that would no longer be acceptable. My brother Joe and sister Grace sat with my dad and diligently taught him how to write his name, "John Xuereb." He took his time and perfected his signature while licking the end of a pencil (I never understood why he needed to lick a leaded pencil). Seeing the results, one could tell it was the scribble of an illiterate person, but overall, it was an accepted signature, and that was all that mattered.

When my daughter Maria was six years of age, and in the first grade, she was learning how to read. One afternoon, while visiting Mom and Dad, Maria was reading a book to them. My dad couldn't get over the fact that this young six-year-old child could read, and here he was at 65 years of age and still couldn't read and could barely write his name. He was surprised at her achievement.

My dad's address book was a sight to see. It was filled with stick figures and drawings of objects and simple markings. I often wonder what happened to that small address book. I wish I had it now to hold, smell and go through it. I know it was pretty beaten up, and the pages were dark from my dad's constantly soiled hands and, of course, it would reek of cigar smell and sulfur from the Ford Motor Company.

Obtaining his driver's license would be virtually impossible on his own. The help of translators accompanying the applicant wasn't heard of back in the 50s, but bribery was. It was somewhat easy for one to pay a little extra for a full-fledged driver's license. What I didn't understand was how someone like my dad could drive safely without being able to read and understand the traffic signs and signals. My mother, on the other hand, learned enough Maltese writing from her two years of schooling to be able to correspond with my sister Marija over the years, especially during that long absence of 14 years. Marija's daughter Josie Attard recently shared with me that her mom and dad went to school together when they were older since neither had the opportunity when they were younger, as chores and the hard life on the farm took precedence. I recall Mother getting a letter every two weeks written in the blue overseas paper that was folded up into an envelope. Mother would immediately drop what she was doing, sit at the dining room table and start to read these letters that always started with, "Hope this letter finds you all in good health as it left us." She would immediately write my sister, also on the blue overseas letter/envelope. She would write and mail it the same day and anxiously wait for my sister to respond. Like clockwork, these letters came and went out over and over again each week. This was their only correspondence.

I felt as if Mother were writing to an imaginary person as I barely knew my sister since she married when I was just fifteen months old, and I had just turned four when we left Malta. We had plenty of pictures, and more were sent over the years, but it bothered me that I never knew my oldest sister Marija, who was 17 years older than me.

✠✠✠✠✠

Overseas telephone calls were very costly, and the equipment was faulty more often than not. If you could ever get through it, it sounded like you were talking through a water tunnel, with much delay and lack of audibility. My sister Marija would never write of a pregnancy but rather announce at a later date that a baby was born on such a date. I found this so unusual, but I guess things were very private and not spoken of as easily as they are today.

✠✠✠✠✠

With computers so abundant now, I sit and imagine what life between Mother and our sister would have been like if they had access to a computer. Can you imagine, with a click of a button, they could share pictures and even talk to each other live via the webcam, Skype, Facebook, and all the other social media options out there today? Can't you just see and picture them on Facetime? I often think that computers came some 50 years too late for them.**

Death certificate of Dad's Mom Marija Sant Xuereb.

DAD'S TAXI, BUS, AND JEEP

Just before the war, my father acquired a taxi cab; how, I'm not sure, but my mother would tell me how excited my father was; he would drive up and down the streets giving his friends a lift. My mother tells the story of her walking up the Mosta curve with her two young girls, Marija and Grace, going down to Burrmarrad when, all of a sudden, she hears someone repeatedly honking and honking. Well, it turns out to be my father in this taxi cab with a car full of ladies, not just any ladies but ladies of the night from Hamrun. Mother said she was furious; one, because he didn't stop to give his family a ride, and two, because of the ladies he was seen with. My dad merely said he couldn't pass up the fare, although he never seemed to bring home any money.

✠✠✠✠✠

Another interesting vehicle story is the time my dad owned a city bus. I don't know how this bus fell into my dad's possession, but I don't believe this ownership lasted too long. Dad did the driving, and Joe Gatt, his son-in-law, was the money taker. Mother tells me that during the first week of business, my father would come home with a hat full of coins, but that slowly dwindled as he would justify his lack of funds by saying, "But those were my friends. I couldn't charge them."

✠✠✠✠✠

Dad got ahold of a Jeep. Mother loved that jeep; she was just learning how to drive on the farm and felt empowered in that vehicle, but there's an interesting part of the jeep story that I heard from my brother Joe. The police came to confiscate this vehicle that my dad had hidden under a pile of hay. He was notified by his police friend, George Camilleri, from Luqa, but he was stationed in St. Paul's Bay.

Without hesitation, my dad took and bit the vehicle identification plate right off the dashboard with his bare teeth. Joe, just a young boy, couldn't believe his eyes and stood there with his mouth dropped open in amazement during this unbelievable and most unlikely task.

Note: George Camilleri January 11, 1927-September 13, 2017

WORLD WAR II

Germany started the Second World War in September 1939. Malta, because of its strategic position in the Mediterranean, was soon in the thick of things. Malta was bombed very heavily by the German and Italian air forces – night and day -- and after two and a half years of never-ending air raids, the bravery, heroism, and sacrifice of its people were recognized.

Malta was the most bombed area during World War II. King George VI awarded the Maltese people the George Cross Medal on April 15, 1942. (Note: Malta is the only commonwealth under English rule to receive that honor during World War II). Mother would often say that Victor, born in 1940, started the war and Frank, born in 1942, ended it for Malta. During those years, Mother said she got pretty proficient at recognizing if it was an Italian or German plane flying overhead while they occupied an air raid shelter. Can you imagine taking cover in an air raid shelter with small children let alone a baby? The first bombing attack by the Italians was on the 11th of June 1940. April of 1942 was the worst month, with 6,700 tons of bombs were dropped on the Grand Harbour area.

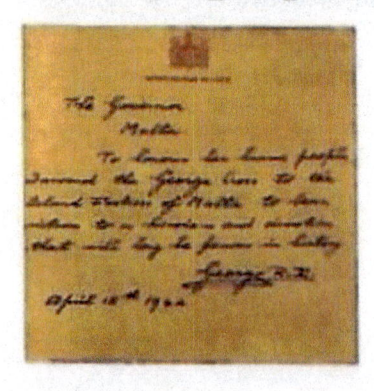

Mother speaks of a small shed near the farm. During World War II, the men in the area, including my dad, would gather in this small building and gamble, probably rounds of (Trentun) thirty-one. One particular day, my mom asked my dad, basically begging him for some unknown reason, to stay home, which he did. To everyone's shocking surprise, that shed and a sudden blast of gunfire hit the men in it. Thank God my dad listened to my mother.

The Opera House during World War II

The Opera House before World War II

MARIJA AND JOE'S MARRIAGE

My oldest sister Marija married Joe Gatt, tal Gzejjer, on September 19, 1948. I was 15 months old. They wanted to marry earlier, but Mother said at least wait till I have the baby. The Gatts lived directly across from us, separated by a creek. They too had a large family. My sister was the oldest of seven, and Joe Gatt was the third oldest of eight. Marija and Joe would spend time talking during breaks. My dad and Joe's dad, Salvu, thought it would be a perfect match. So, the wedding preparation began. Marija told me of the beautiful bed linens being part of her dowry. These linens were generally used to decorate the bed during the baptism of a new baby. Joe laughed one day, telling me they were in the linen closet more than they were used and displayed.

✠✠✠✠✠

The marriage took place in Mosta Rotunda Church. Just a few years back, my sister Marija told me she was married on the side altar of St. Joseph, as weddings were never performed in front of the large main altar of the Rotunda. She said she wore a beautiful burgundy-colored dress and had an exquisite wedding.

Gatt family: Josephine Attard, Jimmy, Sam, Doris Scicluna, Charlie, John, sitting Marija & Joe.

Note: Joe Gatt passed away on July 11, 2012, just over two years after his wife, our sister Marija's passing. I truly believe his love for her was so strong that life meant nothing to him after her death. They were inseparable; they did everything together. Marija never ate dinner until Joe came home from work, and then she would always sit at his side. I remember watching Joe cut out the center of a watermelon, the sweetest part, and place it on her plate, just one of his small deeds of endearment. Joe once told me how Marija walked a long distance to bring him his afternoon tea and how he loved her for that. I believe Marija never made a trip to Detroit to visit her family because they were so close, and the thought of separation for even a short time was something she was unwilling to undertake. For a man who never felt ill during his busy, rough years of building up his company, "Gatt Brothers Construction," he was in and out of the hospital four times during the last six months of his life, starting with a fall, losing weight, developing phenomena, and his heart starting to deteriorate. He tried to carry on but found it much too difficult without his Marija, even with all the love and care from his 6 children, 11 grandchildren, and 7 great-grandchildren.

DAD GOING BACK TO MALTA

When we left for America, Dad promised Mother that he would go back for Marija and her family. Dad kept his promise, the separation would be temporary, and he flew back in 1954 and tried to persuade Joe to bring his young family to America without success, as Joe was just starting his construction business. Dad even bought the house next door from us on Baker St. for Marija and her family in preparation for their coming to America.

I've explained that Mother never wanted to leave; she often said she couldn't blame Joe for wanting to stay in the country he loved with his family and near his parents and siblings.

Marija, sitting with grandchildren: Francesca Scicluna, d/o Doris, Jason Gatt, s/o Sam, Joseph Gatt, s/o Jimmy, Luana Scicluna Farrugia, d/o Doris, James Gatt, s/o Jimmy. Middle row: Claudine Gatt, d/o John, Kristina Gatt Bonavia, d/o Charlie, great-granddaughter Mariah Gatt d/o Chris on the end, Jevon Gatt, s/o John, Chris Gatt, s/o Sam with Daughter Michela Gatt and his sister Nathalie Gatt, front row: Marija holding great-granddaughter Catrina Brincat d/o Claudine, Kurt Gatt behind her, s/o Charlie, great-grandson Luke Gatt s/o Jevon, and Karl Gatt (hiding in the back) s/o Claudine. Born after this photo, great-grandson Sebastian Gatt s/o Jevon Gatt, great-granddaughter Mara Farrugia, d/o Luana Scicluna Farrugia, great-granddaughter Morgan Nosenzo Gatt d/o Chris Gatt, great, great-granddaughter Siena Mae Gatt d/o Mariah Gatt, great granddaughter Carla Farrugia d/o Luana Scicluna Farrugia and great granddaughter Bettina Bonavia d/o Kristina Gatt.

["d/o"=daughter of, "s/o"=son of].

Marija Assunta (18) and Guisseppi Gatt (20) marriage September 19, 1948

At the Church of the Rotunda, Mosta, Malta.

BABY BOY

Years later, in fact, well into my adulthood, my mother told me of a baby boy born in 1949 or 1950. My father was in England, trying his hand at work there and perhaps buying farm equipment, or so my mother thought. The neighbors were often heard laughing and told my mother that my dad wasn't in England but rather in America. She didn't know what to think; she certainly didn't want to believe it. All she knew for certain was the fact that all the farm work without my dad was taking a toll on her. One day, while pulling onions, she felt a sharp pain and found herself having a miscarriage. Mother said it was a beautifully developed baby boy who had the miniature face of my father. She names him Lawrence. From her description, it sounds like she was around four or five months pregnant. The sad part was that my father knew nothing of her pregnancy and she was alone. Mother immediately instructed Grace to go get her sister Marija. Grace was 18 at the time but not married, so it wasn't appropriate for my mother to discuss this matter with her. Grace came back with Marija, and my mother had already wrapped and placed the tiny baby boy in an empty cigar box and instructed Marija to go to the parish church and give the priest the box so that he would know what to do with her baby boy.

ZIJU'S TRAGIC DEATH

The only thing I ever heard about my Zija (aunt) Marija's husband, Gamri (John Mary) Gauci, was a story of his tragic death. Mother often spoke of how his life ended so horribly. He was in the field, which they called "Taflija" (meaning fields of clay) in the area of Ghajn Rihana just left of Burmarrad. He was lifting heavy wheat bundles onto his cart. The rope that he was using snapped and sent him falling only 5-6 feet, apparently causing him to break his neck. This happened on July 14, 1950, but he suffered and eventually died the next day, July 15th, due to his injuries; he was merely 58 years of age. Frances, his daughter, was only 8 years old. Her brother Carmelo was 10 and mentally disabled. Her mother became a widow at 43 years of age. After this tragedy, life was truly rough for my aunt, as well as my cousin. Frances lost her childhood and had to quit school, but managed to teach herself how to read. She had to care for her brother, feed the animals, cook, and get food ready for her mother when she came back after long hours in the fields. Years later, my brother-in-law Joe Gatt from Mosta took me near that area and told me the story once again. He said how senseless his death was to be caused by heavy loads of wheat and an old worn-out rope that should have been thrown out in the trash a long time prior, but farmers used what they had forever.

Cousin Frances and Zija Marija Gauci

THE FAMOUS "MILSA"

I grew up hearing about this thing called milsa time and time again. How I almost died from it. No one seemed to know the word for it in English. It wasn't until I was in high school and decided to do some research that I found out that milsa is Maltese for spleen in English. My brother Joe loved to tell me and anyone who would listen, over and over, how he saved my life when I could have died from this milsa. He would go on and on, and as often as he could, to remind me that I owed him my life. You see, one day, when I was around 2 years of age, I was lying down after a bottle of milk, and my brother Joe, who was 13 at the time, told our mother something was wrong with the baby because her stomach is hard and distended and she looks yellow (jaundice). Mother said no, she just had a bottle, nothing more. Joe insisted that things didn't look right. It got to the point where he made our mother take me to the doctor, where it was diagnosed that I had an infected, swollen spleen. The doctor said it was a good thing that I was brought in when they did or the spleen could have ruptured and caused my death. That made my brother Joe feel like the hero he was. With that diagnosis, a treatment plan was put in place. Over the course of several weeks at a clinic in Floriana, just outside of Valletta, the doctor started me on a series of 12 shots to the neck, which in turn made me quite nauseous. The nurse would lead me into an area that had a drain running along the center of the room, and I would be allowed to vomit it all up. I was very young, but I remembered this continued for what seemed like forever to a young child. In fact, during our first visit back to Malta in 1965, while walking in Floriana, I told my mother this place looked

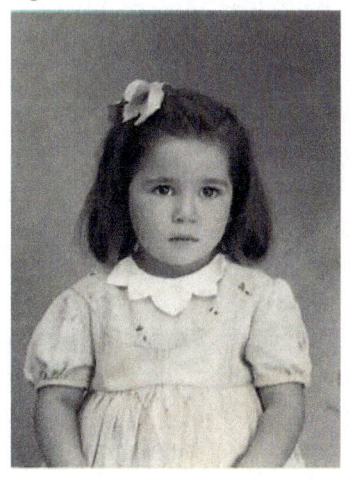

Rena at the age of three.

very familiar to me, and she said it should. She explained how we would walk around the area after getting off the bus and going towards the clinic. She pointed out a grid on the sidewalk where I would stop and look at the little chicks below. Of course, they were no longer there. All these years, I was under the impression that my spleen was dried up since I was told I was too young to have it removed, but recent examinations and X-rays proved that to be false. My spleen is still intact, and it was probably an infection that had caused the spleen to almost rupture. My oncologist recently asked what medication they gave me during those rounds of treatment. All I could tell her was that I just found out what my illness was called in English, let alone know what medication I was given. Due to the severity of this spleen infection, the doctor told my mother that I may never be able to have children as an adult. I heard this all through my school-age years and especially in high school. What a spleen had to do with reproductive organs, I don't know, but then I'm not a doctor and took this at face value and being the truth. This bothered me immensely as I loved children and hoped for a large family. This childhood spleen infection never stopped me since I went on to bear five beautiful, highly intelligent children.

Back row: Chris & Jennifer Suchyta, Theo Williamson & Maria Suchyta, Mr. & Mrs. Marcello/Ana Campos Migliore, Rachael & Dominic (Suchyta) Davis holding Lela Mae, Joseph Suchyta, Front row: Natalia & Nicholas Suchyta children of Chris & Jen, Rena & Fernando Campos, Virgil Davis son of Dominic and Rachael Davis.

Rena's grandchildren who are not included in the photo above:

Fabian Migliore & Xavier Migliore

THE FARM HORSE

As I mentioned earlier, on the farm, we had a horse. This was no ordinary horse. This was a farming/champion racing horse. When he wasn't plowing the fields, he was working as a racehorse in Rabat, Malta. Horse racing in Malta has a long-standing tradition dating back to the 15th century and is still held on Saqqajja Hill at Rabat. The races would start around the Hill in Rabat and go up the incline on the left. One can still see the "Loggia tal-palja" on the balcony (to the right of this photo), where the island's leaders used to watch from. The Palji (prize flags) were brightly colored, and the winners would take these back to their village church, where tribute would be given. During the Feast of St. Peter and St. Paul (Imnarja), our farm horse won the flag in approximately 1949.

In the basement of our Baker Street house stood a brass trophy cup. Ah, the cup! I don't know if it was one of the prized possessions that came with us to America, but unfortunately, it never held a place of honor in our home. I remember, for years, it sat in the basement on an old piano bench used as storage for nails and screws. What pity I had for that cup. If only it could talk. If only I had questioned my parents about its presence years prior. Was it a prize from another horse race? Whatever became of that cup, I do not know, but its vision is clearly in my head. More importantly, whatever happened to that plow/racehorse?

Dad with Joe and his winning horse.

Dad with his jockey.

Dad in front of the farm exercising his horse.

THE MALTESE COW

I can't write about the farm/racehorse in Malta without mentioning our Maltese cow as well. A cow that was bigger than big, a gentle giant, strong and docile. She was a very calm and tranquil cow, also resistant to the sun, whereas other cows can't stand the sun. The domesticated Maltese cow was not a food source but a muscle force with great strength and work capabilities that could carry heavy loads and was also used for plowing. They did not have any fat and were very lean. They did most of the manual labor on a farm, and they only produced enough milk for their calves, even though the milk was very rich. Besides the size of the cow, I especially like the eyes in this picture; she's looking right at you, along with her calf. One distinctive characteristic of the Maltese cows was that they were born with a slightly bent inward hoof. Rumor has it that these large, beautiful creatures were used in building local churches and the unique Maltese prehistoric temples. Some of the animal drawings near the Maltese temples closely resembled the Maltese indigenous cow. Perhaps that is why the older Maltese people say these cows date back to prehistoric times. Unfortunately, the last of the Maltese bulls passed away a few years back, and 100% Maltese cows no longer exist.

The Maltese Cow with her calf, Dad holding them with Joe,

around six years old, kneeling under the cow

✠✠✠✠✠

Note: My brother Joe would never take cream in his tea or coffee; nothing. He revealed to me some time ago that he once saw a cow void in the pail of milk.

HOUSE ON BRISTOL STREET

On August 16, 1950, my father arrived in Detroit, sponsored by Joe Shuereb (who changed his name for clarity). Joe Shuereb, a nephew of my father, had established himself in Detroit since 1948. Additionally, Joseph Sant, an uncle to Joe Shuereb and potentially a nephew of my father's mother, Marianne Sant, played a crucial role in facilitating the arrival. As I mentioned before, my dad was originally headed to Australia, but his nephew Joe wrote and told him he could immediately secure a job upon his arrival in Detroit. My dad found work at Ford Motor Co. Rouge Plant in Dearborn in the Coke Ovens. Coal was shipped into the Rouge using the Rouge River, as well as by rail. The coal was used for the Rouge's giant furnaces, the largest of its kind in the world at that time. This was a hot, dirty, non-environmental existing area of the plant reserved mostly for the immigrants and the illiterate. My dad made $2.00 an hour, an average of $80.00 a week back then, good pay for hard work. While working at Ford, he lived in a boarding house on the Southwest side of Detroit in Corktown owned by Sara, a Maltese lady whose last name we never knew. She rented many rooms to Maltese men awaiting their family's arrival. After only being in the States for a few months, my father managed to purchase a house, 3064 Bristol St., near the Ambassador Bridge and Ste. Anne's Church and School in the Corktown area of Detroit. With a job and house in place, it was now time for the family to join him. Upon our arrival in Detroit in June of 1951, at the Michigan Central Train Station, once the tallest train station in the world. The group of seven Xuerebs was greeted by my father, who immediately told my mother that he was about to have someone write to her to say he was returning to Malta and to not bother coming to the USA. My mother was furious, and she immediately told him, "Then why didn't you say anything, making this voyage that I wanted no part of with six kids and to hear this." Not the best thing to say to a woman who just made a 13-day voyage and a train ride with 6 children. The train station located at 2405 West Vernor Highway was not far from this house on Bristol St. We all piled into his car, all seven of us plus my dad. When we arrived at the house he had purchased for us, my dad had a pound cake waiting for us. I don't believe we ate on the train; we were so hungry that we devoured that cake in no time at all.

✠✠✠✠✠

I always called my dad "Tata," Maltese for dad. It wasn't until I was in my 30s that my mother told me to stop calling him that because it was a term used by very young children. I'm sorry, but that's what I called him for years, and it felt very comfortable to me. I continued calling him "Tata" or "Ta" for years.

✠✠✠✠✠

My siblings attended Ste. Anne's School in the fall, only to find the language barrier so difficult that they were all held back. Grace, twenty, and Joe, fifteen, were too old for this school and eventually attended English night classes. I, on the other hand, was only four years old and had a whole year to learn English on the streets while playing with the friends I had made in the neighborhood.

✠✠✠✠✠

My mother never grew fond of this neighborhood and asked my father to find a house even closer to a school and church. I don't remember much about this house other than that it had a big potbelly furnace off the living room near the kitchen. I found this hunk of metal in a house very strange, especially coming from an island with no central heat, no type of heat at all. I do remember leaving with my new friends to play, and my mother always worried about where I had run off to. My dad sold this house just before it was demolished for the new I-75 freeway running near the Ambassador Bridge.

HANGING CLOTHES IN THE WINTER

When we first arrived in Detroit, it was the month of June, and mother hung her wash outside as she had done all her life. The only thing different was the climate when the winter months approached. In Malta, one can generally hang their clothes to dry year-round, but here in Detroit, that would prove to be a problem during the freezing winter months. A neighbor watched my mom outside in the cold, hanging her clothes on the line. She finally informed my mom, the best she could with the language barrier, that one does not hang clothes to dry outside in the winter. My mom proceeded to take the clothes down and found them to be as stiff as a board. She took them inside to thaw and decided to drape them over the big pot belly furnace, which was a new concept to her, as there were no furnaces in Malta. This large, round piece of metal sat in the dining room of the house; unfortunately, as the clothes started to dry, they also started to smoke as they lay on the furnace past any reasonable time. From that day forward, mother would only hang her clothes indoors during inclement weather.

Mother and Rena hanging clothes in the basement of the house on Baker.

We tried to introduce slacks to my Mother. We bought her a pair of blue ones in the 60s. She was a good sport about it and wore them a couple of times, but it wasn't her thing; she almost felt embarrassed. Her church friends wore slacks but not my Mom. She preferred her house dresses.

BAKER STREET HOUSE

Dad honored Mom's request for a house near a church and school. Every day on his way home from work at Ford Rough Plant in Dearborn, he would turn off Vernor Highway, the main road, onto neighborhood streets. He slowly drove up and down, looking for "For Sale" signs on the lawns. One day, he happened upon a man pounding in a "For Sale" sign. How perfect, just a block away from Holy Redeemer Church and School, just as Mom requested. He immediately approached the seller before he was even done pounding the sign into the ground. They came to an agreement of $9,950.00 on a land contract over a handshake. Immediately, my dad suggested they go to Elsea Real Estate on Fort St., just a mile away, to seal the deal on paper. Dad gave the Seller, Mr. Monteau, $2,000.00 down with an agreement of $64.00 monthly payments. This would eventually become the practice and routine for any further home-buying endeavors my dad would encounter. He couldn't wait to tell my mother the good news.

Dolores. Frank, Victor, Grace & Dad

My dad quickly sold the house at 3064 Bristol St., and we moved into 5840 Baker St. on the Southwest side of Detroit just a mile or so from our first home. Eva Fitzpatrick and her family lived next door to us and upstairs from her mother, Mrs. Perez; she told us later that there was word that the house was going to be sold, and she was waiting, for what seemed like forever, for the neighbor to put the house up on the market to be sold. But my dad was at the right place at the right time and certainly didn't waste any time dwelling over small matters like waiting so Mother could see it. He was never one to dwell on things; he made his decision and acted quickly. It was a good size and consisted of a living room, dining room, two bedrooms, a bath, a kitchen, and a full basement, but with eight Xuereb members about to move in, my dad eventually converted the back porch into a kitchen and made a bedroom out of the former kitchen. I remember when my dad put up walls to create the hallway, almost immediately, there was scratching and meowing behind one wall, from a cat that must of fell in during the night during construction. My dad couldn't figure out how to help free this poor creature without tearing up all his hard-handy work. If I'm not mistaken, I think my dad thought of making that wall the cats final resting place but mother, a cat lover, wouldn't have any part of that. Eventually, dad ended up cutting out a hole to free the young cat who jumped out and ran for his life. The upstairs of the Baker Street house consists of three bedrooms, a kitchen, and a bath. We generally had three Maltese borders living there for years. Later, it was rented as an upper flat.

Dad made a lot of changes to the house over time. I remember my dad contracting Mr. Charles Caruana, known as Shorty, the Maltese man who lived down the street from us on Campbell Street and who also had a large family of seven children; his daughter Carmela was in my class at Holy Redeemer and still a great friend. We had these beautiful tulip-designed leaded glass sliding doors between our living room and dining room that my dad had Mr. Caruana permanently push into the walls, remove the "old" solid wood trim, and replace with a more modern

Mother, Grace, Dad & Rena

archway. Even as young as I was, I could not for the life of me figure out the purpose of hiding such exquisite, beautiful doors.

The floors were covered with linoleum in a heavy flowered print, with door tracks for the sliding doors still in the center. The walls were also wallpapered with large plant leaves. Thinking back, there was nothing subtle about the interiors of homes back then. Wallpaper was very fashionable, along with bold prints and colors. Eventually, my dad had the wallpapered walls painted over, and till the day my mother left her home almost fifty years later, we never did remove that wallpaper from the walls; we always just added a fresh coat of paint. In the living room, two decorative gas-burning accent scones above the couch hung on the wall; my dad had those removed as well. In between these accents, we had a mirror with a picture of soft pink flamingos amidst an array of green ferns. Funny, how pinks and green came back into style years later in the '80s and, especially, any mention of pink flamingos. My dad went on to add the mission brick front after admiring what another neighbor down the street did to his house. This was done shortly after adding the new long porch he had just erected, the big picture window my mom could sit and look out of when she wasn't sitting on her new porch. As my mom got older, she spent hundreds of hours reading her Maltese books (sent to her by her daughter Marija in Malta) by this window and doing her "neighborhood watch." She thought her big window had a one-way view, so she sometimes failed to realize that everyone could see her as well. Like clockwork, she could tell you what time a neighbor left home and what time they returned. Mother would have a dozen questions and comments for anyone who would listen. Mother loved her vegetable garden; she was so happy when she could work the soil. She instinctually knew what to plant to bring it to its peak; farming was in her blood. Visions of old refrigerator bins full of dirt and hens and chicks come to mind, and those plants were everywhere along the back kitchen wall lined with makeshift benches. She loved hanging her clothes outside on breezy days. Chin-ups on clothes poles were my favorite pastime. Mother enjoyed playing badminton in the middle of the street on spring/summer nights; she was very good at it.

My dad even put in a sprinkling system that wasn't heard of back then. He raised rabbits in the garage, and just outside near the garage, he had a fig tree, not just any fig tree, but one brought back as a twig from Malta. That tree produced large succulent figs, most likely with the help of the rabbits just on the other side. Every year before the winter frost, he would painstakingly bend the fig tree down carefully so as not to snap the trunk, cover it with hay, then drape a tarp over it. Since fig trees do not do well in harsh Michigan winters, this had to be done routinely every year. Come spring, when all chance of frost has passed, the tree is uncovered and allowed to flourish and once again provide us with an abundance of fresh figs during the August and September months. My dad also loved the Dahlia bulbs that he planted year after year along the fence. Every year, he would winterize them in the basement in the sand under the new kitchen. My dad had several fruit trees that he enjoyed planting and caring for over the years. He was upset one day when teenage "punks" were picking and throwing the fruit and breaking windows; actually, he used ten times worse names for them that I can't repeat. I don't know when I saw my dad so angry. Those peach and plum trees came down so fast after years of tender care. Such a shame he took great pride in his success at grafting those trees. He was good at it. Overall, my mother was happy in that house on Baker St. from 1952 till 1996. Almost fifty years in the same house with the same telephone number. The stories those walls could tell. Mother and I would often take our evening walks. Generally, we would walk down Campbell to Porter onto a bakery off the side street and purchase long sugar-glazed donuts for a nickel, so they would be good and fresh out of the oven. We continued walking and turned and came home after a mile or so. Another route, especially on Tuesdays, would be to go straight down Vernor to Clark

Dad with his fig tree

Park, where the band would be playing in full uniform at the band shelter; we would enjoy the music before heading back, another mile or more of a walk. Some Saturdays, we would make a quick turn down Junction Street and make a house payment at a local mom-and-pop store that the sellers of our Baker Street house owned, and then we would venture to the Stratford Theater to enjoy a movie. Around 1972, that theater was sold and only featured Spanish-speaking movies. Mother would still want to go and take in a movie, but I explained to her that they are now in Spanish, and we couldn't understand the movie; her only reply was, "So, I could barely understand it when it was in English."

✠✠✠✠✠

Baker Street was a good small block with great neighbors. Although I think it was my dad's dream to buy out the whole block of Baker Street. He bought the house next to us shortly after we moved in. This house he bought in 1953 for my sister Marija and her family just before he returned to Malta to bring them to Detroit as he had promised. All the visas and papers were in order, but my dad came back alone. My brother-in-law Joe Gatt didn't want to leave Malta, his family, and his construction company that was just starting up. My mother said she couldn't blame him as she never wanted to leave Malta either.

✠✠✠✠✠

My dad went on to buy the house next door to Marija's house, as we called it. Mrs. Kehoe lived alone for years before passing away in her late 90s. My dad immediately bought and set out to turn this beautiful old house into a two-unit dwelling as he did to Marija's house; after all, he was in the landlord business when not working at Ford. I don't recall my dad sitting and relaxing much. He would come home from a hard day of work in the coke ovens only to go out to work on a new rental he just purchased. Many a day, I didn't even see him before he left again, but I knew he came home because of the cigar and sulfur smell that lingered in the house. Tuesday at 8 p.m. is the only time I ever saw my dad stop, sit, and watch his favorite program, The Red Skeleton Show, a comedy that would relax and unwind him for a short time. He had purchased a large house on Dragoon about three city blocks away and asked my mother if she wanted to move there; of course, her immediate reaction was "NO." she wanted nothing to do with a house that far from church and school. He went to work to convert that house into a three-unit dwelling.

✠✠✠✠✠

My dad once brought home pigeons that hung out at Ford Motor Co. Rouge Plant. While my mom was preparing the birds, she saw they were just filled with steel pellets, not edible for sure. My mom and dad had a good laugh.

Job's Tear Seeds, just ripening, then harvested.

Victor brought home seeds, Job's Tears Seeds, that the nuns had given him and asked my mom to plant them. They grew into small beads that we harvested, and Victor took them back to the nuns who made rosaries out of them.

The finished product: a rosary made of the seeds..

Josephine Vella, Dad, Rena, Tommy Vella, Dolores & Carmen Vella. These very special neighbors lived around the corner from us.

A man with a camera, a tripod, a pony, and a sombrero would go through the neighborhood taking pictures for $2.00. Rena was lucky enough to have her picture taken one Saturday afternoon.

Mom watering while Rena does chin-ups.

Mother & Dolores on Baker Street.

Dolores & Rena in high school uniforms.

Dolores & Rena leveling the new porch of the house on Baker

Mother & Rena with Penny the dog on the front porch of the house on Baker.

Frank and Victor enjoying the American way of dressing.

Dad and Mom taking a lunch break.

Dad sprucing the front of the original porch (1953).

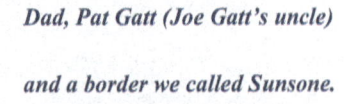

Dad, Pat Gatt (Joe Gatt's uncle) and a border we called Sunsone.

Mom and Dad on the front steps.

Nanna with Maria and Joe Suchyta.

The three houses on Baker Street which Dad owned.

SATURDAYS

A typical Saturday in our household would consist of my mother coming to our bedroom door around 8:30 a.m. and softly remarking, "Inti se tqum?" "Are you getting up?" At 8:45 a.m., she'd reappear by our door and ask "Qed tqum jew!?" "Are you getting up or what!?" in a harsher voice. Shortly after, she would once again stand at our door for the third and last time in a loud announcing voice and say: "il disgha, qum minn ghem!" "It's 9 a.m. Get up from there!" With that command, my sister Dolores and I would jump out of bed from a deep sleep, have our morning tea, and divide the house-cleaning chores. In the early afternoon, my mother and I would walk to Camilleri's Market, the local Maltese-owned market on Junction and Eldred, about 10 minutes away. We would take a pull cart and buy an average of six bags of groceries, canned goods, and meat for an average of $20.00 for the week. Fresh fruit and vegetables would be bought from two Italian vendors who came through the local streets in their open trucks a few times a week. Fresh Italian bread was also delivered to the house twice a week. I also remember the horse-drawn Twin Pines milk truck years earlier, delivering right to the house. After dinner, which my mother had prepared in the morning, we would relax in front of the television and settle in for the 9 p.m. Saturday Night Movie. No sooner did we get comfortable than you could hear my mother calling from the kitchen just down the long hallway, "Min se jghinni?". "Who's going to help me?" This is when Dolores and I would argue over who held that rabbit the week prior. My mother was ready and waiting, so one of us would give in, although we tried to alternate assisting my mother on Saturday's rabbit preparation for Sunday's dinner. This would consist of a live rabbit from my dad's garage pen being brought into the newspaper-covered kitchen floor. My mother would cuddle and soothe the rabbit for a minute, making sure it wasn't a pregnant female, and with a blink of an eye, she instantly held him by his hind legs and gave him a karate chop to the neck with one blow, the rabbit was dead and ready to be prepared. My sister or I would have the "honor" of holding him by his hind legs so my mom could do her thing. As she masterfully began to dissect the poor rabbit, who would soon become Sunday's dinner, she would never fail to point out the thin, blackened inch-long spleen (milsa) as she carefully removed it from the rabbit's cavity while remarking, "This is what you almost died from." I can't tell you how many rabbit spleens I have seen over the years following my mother's brief explanation.

This also reminds me of the first time my Irish-Scottish sister-in-law Ginger McIntyre happened upon the Sunday dinner rabbit preparation ritual. Ginger and Joe were newlyweds back in 1954 and decided to come over for a visit one Saturday evening while this meal preparation was going on. Ginger happened into the kitchen and was beside herself, going on and on about this beautiful white furry creature having pink eyes, but come Sunday afternoon, when they came over for dinner, my mother said, "All the fuss, but she has no problem eating the poor white rabbit." This meal preparation was second nature to us, a way of life in a Maltese household, but to an American-born person, I guess it would seem a little strange and barbaric to walk into such a scene.

✠✠✠✠✠

I have to tell you of the time mother had on a striped dress. Dad didn't say a word, went to church, and when he returned, he couldn't hold back any longer; he took one look at mother and told her to take off that striped dress. You look like you just got out of prison. That was an ongoing joke for years. Every time someone wore a striped shirt, someone would make the prison remark.

Ginger McIntyre Xuereb

Rena & Ginger Playing checkers.

Dad and our first television set

My dad with our first TV. We had to make sure it was off when my dad approached the front steps. I guess electricity was high even back then. Later we bought a film of plastic paper with different colors on it. We attached it to the TV, and voila, we had a color TV.

Sunday dinner at Mom and Dad's house on Baker.

The boys at the house on Baker. Front row: Joey Xuereb, Tony Vella, Johnny Xuereb.

Back row: John and Ed Vella, Buzzy, and Roddy Xuereb.

The Vellas are Grace's boys and the Xuerebs are Joe's boys.

READER'S DIGEST

Somehow, just short of moving into the Baker St. house, we started receiving The Reader's Digest. No one seems to recall placing an order of what seemed to be a weekly paperback, especially when our household of eight could barely write English, let alone read it, yet I remember this paperback automatically being delivered very often, perhaps even weekly, and they were everywhere in the house. Why no one ever canceled is a mystery as well, perhaps no one thought we could, or perhaps we carried over our old island rule of once an item is purchased, it's yours, no questions, no refunds. The only one who was able to read these paperbacks was Ginger; after all, she was an American girl born and bred.

✠✠✠✠✠

I remember years later when my brother Joe was going on and on over something very petty. My mother stopped him in his tracks and said, "Who died and made you Nixon." (referring to President Richard Nixon)

✠✠✠✠✠

Two sayings I heard mother repeat all the time:

1. Ghajnejn akbar mill-zaqqik . Your eyes are bigger than your stomach, and

2. Wara d-dahk jigi biki. After laughter comes crying.

Mother enjoyed a good afternoon cup of coffee made in her percolator coffee pot. She'd fill the pot and wait for it to perk. The smell of coffee lingered throughout the house.

MEASLES AND CHICKEN POX

Shortly after we moved into our Baker St. house, two types of rashes invaded our household. Some of us developed measles, and the rest of us were stricken with chicken pox. Mother was terrified and kept us locked up in the house with curtains drawn. She feared the health inspector coming to the house to eventually quarantine our home as they would have done in Malta. It was only years later, in 1975, after giving birth to my son Dominic, that I found out I had German measles. I had a friend who casually told me her son contracted German measles; being pregnant, I informed my doctor that I was most likely exposed, and he told me not to fear; he ran tests and found that I already had German measles as a child.

✠✠✠✠✠

My mother, sometime in her life, had chicken pox as well, perhaps at the same time as her kids or perhaps in her childhood. While in the nursing home during the last years of her life, she developed shingles, which is a very painful rash and only appears after prior exposure to chicken pox. We tried everything to get her to stop scratching. We even put oven mitts on her hands that we secured very well, we thought, but she always managed to wiggle out of them. Thankfully, she didn't seem to experience much pain due to her dementia.

✠✠✠✠✠

Whenever her children were sick, Mother, without fail, would always bring home from Rose's Drug Store, which was located just down the street, a Hershey's chocolate bar, a small ten-cent bag of chips, and a Twinkie. I did not like the cream filling in the Twinkie, but I never mentioned it to my mom. I greatly appreciated the treats.

ABANDONED HOUSE ON BAKER

When we moved into 5840 Baker St. in Southwest Detroit, there was one eyesore on the perfectly manicured short block of homes. This house was fully furnished but empty, very strange, and the windows were all intact in the beginning, so we could easily look into the house. The outside of the house was wooden and grey/black in colors, worn over the years and in bad need of a fresh coat of paint. We didn't know the history of this big house that looked as if it housed an active family. Shirley Fernandez lived next door and said it was vacant even back in the 40s. She said the house didn't even have electricity but rather gas lamps, and when the owners died, the heirs were in court over ownership. Eventually, they also died, and because of greed, this charming house stood out like a sore thumb until it was deemed dangerous and uninhabitable and torn down in the '80s. Such a shame, it appeared to have so much warmth and character. Frank Fernandez, who lived on the other side, bought the lot and made a beautiful space.

The abandoned eyesore on Baker Street. Two of Frank's friends waiting for him.

FIRST SHOWER

Around 1977 or so, my mom and dad took their first vacation together outside of visiting Malta. Mother spoke of visiting Florida and how relaxed they were, taking one slow day at a time. Dad tried his hand at fishing near the motel they stayed at, going to the dog races, and just enjoying life. After 10 days or so, when they decided it was time to come home, mother jokingly told my dad, while they were in the airport," Wouldn't it be nice to go see Dolores and her family in New York?" all of a sudden, my dad disappeared for a short time. While on the plane, my mother heard the captain announce they would soon be landing in New York. Mother turned and asked my dad what he had done, and he responded, "You said you wanted to go see Dolores." Luckily, my mother had her small telephone book in her purse. Dolores' husband, Stoney, picked them up from the airport. Stoney, being a lifer in the U.S. Army, was recently stationed in New York with his family. While at their apartment, mother decided to take a shower, her first shower ever. Growing up on Baker Street, we only had a bathtub, never a shower, and I'm sure during her time in Malta, they had no bathroom, let alone a tub and shower. So, Mother is in the tub, turns on the water, and doesn't know what to do. She was drowning in water, water coming at her in full force. She told me she didn't know what else to do but try to block the water as it was hitting her face. When they arrived back in Detroit, she was going over the story and gesturing with her hands about how she was trying to dodge the water from the shower. Just the way she was explaining it to me made it very comical. She was laughing while telling me the story, but I'm sure she wasn't laughing at the time.

MOTHER'S HEALTH PROBLEMS

Mother started having female health problems, likely stemming from being pregnant for most of twenty years. Learning that Josephine was on her way to the U.S.A., her doctor in Malta suggested she wait until she arrived in the States to have surgery, citing better surgeons, hospitals, and care. The doctor inserted a hook (as Mother described it) and lifted her uterus in place until she was able to address the situation in the States. Unfortunately, it wasn't as easy as the doctor made it sound. Once in the States, my father's employer, Ford Motor Co., informed him that health insurance for his wife and children would not start until nine months after enrollment. This caused my mother to bear the uterus hook for several more months while she made weekly visits to the doctor, who, in turn, also had her wear a corset girdle that this American doctor prescribed for her. This corset looked like something out of the 1800s: flesh-colored, long, with stiff rib cords running along the length. It would rest under her breastbone down to her hips. It looked very uncomfortable, but mother never complained. Every morning, we would have to help her put it on and then lace it very tightly in the back.

Once her hysterectomy surgery was taken care of, my mother recalls her stay in the hospital, an area unfamiliar to her, and not being able to communicate with the staff made it even more unbearable. She was very uncomfortable and couldn't explain the pain she was experiencing; she felt very much alone. She recalls repeatedly saying, "I can't, I can't," in a very broken accent, and no one understood what the problem was. To say she was very frustrated was an understatement. Coming home after several days in the hospital, I don't remember my mom taking the proper time to heal and recuperate; after all, she had a family to care for.

Years later, some thirty years later, she was once again experiencing pain in the abdominal area. After extensive examination and testing, we were told that mother did not have a total hysterectomy as we previously thought; she, in fact, only had her uterus removed back in 1952, leaving her ovaries, which were now causing her problem. One ovary was the size of a grapefruit and had to be removed. The other was dried up like a prune. My poor mother has endured so much pain and various surgeries over the years, and never once did I hear her complain.

One awful time I remember is the hiatal hernia she had developed in the 80s; she was also diagnosed with diverticulitis. This condition worsened when her home was broken into one early morning while living alone on Baker Street after my father's death. Four young juveniles were going around, terrifying older people in the neighborhood. They obtained access through a basement window while dawn was just approaching one snowy wintery morning. They kicked in the entry door, tied her up in a chair, and taped her mouth while they went around and helped themselves. They mocked and terrified her while laughing throughout the ordeal, but once they left, she was able to free herself enough to call my brother Joe, who immediately called the police. Once I arrived and without any fear of retaliation, she insisted on going to the 4th precinct police station, where I watched in pride and amazement while she bravely picked out one juvenile face after another through their mug shots. With her helpful observation and quick recall, the police and their team of dogs were able to confirm and arrest these young men who left their scent and shoe prints in the light snow at the local McDonald's. She courageously went to the trial and took the witness stand while they smirked and laughed as they sat handcuffed, staring her down the whole time. My brother Joe wanted to get out of his seat and rip them apart. They had no remorse whatsoever. In the end, they were all sentenced to a working farm for juveniles, but from that time on, mother feared sleeping alone, and who could blame her? My kids would then take turns spending the nights with her.

The horrific part of this was her paraesophageal hiatal hernia tore and worsened from the trauma, and surgery was needed to repair the damage. Unfortunately, back in the 80s, laparoscopic surgery did not exist. Once again, Mother had to go through a very invasive procedure that did not go well. Needless to say, the hernia was repaired but only after leaving her with a six-inch-long incision. The staples did not adhere, and she ended up with a large crater that needed to be packed and changed constantly. Diligent and careful attention was required for months until it could heal naturally without infection. In the end, she was left with an ugly scar and two large protruding herniated lumps under her breastbone, along with a 3mm staple that fell into the incision area during surgery at Memorial Hospital in Downtown Detroit. This hospital no longer exists.

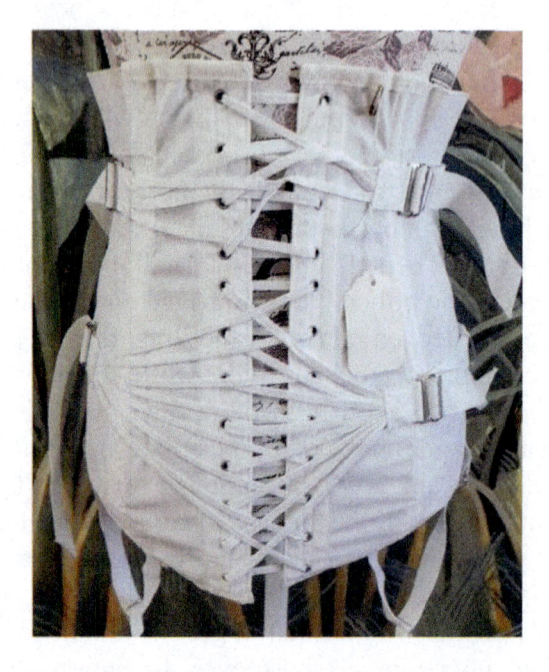

The corset that was ordered by mother's doctor and she endured it before her surgery. Since it laced in the back, we had to strap her in tightly every morning.

GRACE AND JOE

Our neighbor, Shirley Fernandez, who lived directly across the street from us in the white house, worked at the Fort Shelby Hotel in downtown Detroit. In the fall of 1952, shortly after moving into Baker St., she was able to secure my sister Grace a job there as a bus girl who cleared and cleaned the tables for the waitresses, and my brother Joe also worked there as a bus boy who carried the dirty dishes to the kitchen to be washed. They both enjoyed working there, but shortly after, my dad managed to secure both of them jobs at Ford Motor Co. They both worked on the assembly line.

✠✠✠✠✠

Grace worked afternoons and Joe the midnight shift. Grace would take the Baker bus to and from work. That is where she met her husband, Emanuel (Leli, or Manuel) Vella, who also worked at Ford. He stuck out his tongue at her one day, and that's all it took. When she invited him home to meet the family, Emanuel recalls me shouting over and over, "iżżewweġ," meaning, "Get Married." Dinner consisted of a nice stuffed chicken that my mom prepared, but when my dad went to carve that bird, it had a mind of its own and decided to fly off the table. Mother was so embarrassed, but Manuel picked up the bird and proceeded to carve. We laughed about it later.

While dating, I, or generally my sister Dolores, accompanied them at all times, even though Grace was twenty-five years of age. We shared many Sunday afternoons on Belle Isle. I often reminded Emanuel that it was my outburst at the dinner table that sealed the deal. For their wedding on April 28, 1956, I was chosen to be the flower girl; maybe that was my repayment.

As a nine-year-old, I felt so beautiful, all dressed up in my pretty dress; on the other hand, my sister Dolores didn't feel the way I did since my mother had to leave her home with a nurse. You see, Dolores had a fever of well over 100 due to tonsillitis. A nurse was brought in to care for Dolores for the sum of $20.00; she cared for her the entire day. When we came home to check on her in the afternoon, there was a tall pile of sheets behind the door. I think every bedsheet we owned. The nurse changed the bedding quite often since Dolores was breaking into a cold sweat.

Joe was only sixteen when he started working for Ford Motor Co. My dad changed the year on his birth certificate from 1936 to 1934 so that he could meet the eighteen-year age requirement. Joe eventually admitted to Ford Motor Co. on his retirement, after thirty years of service, that he was a mere forty-six years of age and that he was only sixteen when he started. Management told him that this made him the youngest person to retire from Ford with thirty years of service. Joe met his blond, Virginia (Ginger) McIntyre, on the Bob-Lo boat one Sunday afternoon. A young man on the ship was following Ginger, so she immediately saw Joe standing alone on the boat. She ran and stood by him as if they were together. It all started there. They were married on September 25, 1954.

Note: Grace passed away on May 27, 2013, after several years of battling dementia. May she be reunited with her daughters, our parents, sister Marija, and brother Joe. Grace and Emanuel lost two daughters over the years. Josephine just shortly after birth in 1960 on Christmas Day, and Catherine (pictured on the left) on January 7, 1970, at the young age of 6 ½ years when she was struck by a car on the way to school. We lost their dad, Manuel, on July 7, 2017. Brother Joe passed on March 20 2010, just a week after

sister Marija. We recently lost Ginger on May 5th, 2022. His second wife Theresa Xuereb passed on May 12, 2022, just a week later. Cousin John Xuereb passed on May 2, 2016, & Steve St. Angelo passed on October 19, 2018.

April 28, 1956   Rena, Dad, Theresa Vella, Joe, Grace & Manuel Vella, Caruana couple & Tommy Vella

Note: The Caruana couple (don't recall their first names) were in a fatal car crash just after Grace's wedding.

Rena, Caruana, Grace and Tessie.

Rena Xuereb & Tommy Vella.

Grace, Manuel, and Dad at the house on Baker St.

Carmina Fernandez and her sister-in-law Shirley Fernandez.

Steve St. Angelo & wife Ida, Ginger & Joe, Grace, and Cousin John Xuereb.

Ginger with Joe.

Steve St. Angelo, Ginger & Joe.

Vella's children: Ed holding David, John, Larry, Carmen, Tony, and Cathy.

Grace with Ed.

Ginger & Joe with five of their six kids: Carmen, John, Joe, Anthony (Buzz) & Rod

Dad with Rod, Buzz, Joe, John, Carmen and Jimmy. Dad would ask if you want a watch, and he would bite you slightly on the wrist and leave teeth marks. Grandkids were terrified. Dad thought it was funny.

Joe, John, Rod, and Jimmy at Duly's Coney Island in our old neighborhood in Southwest Detroit.

Ginger Xuereb with her six children: Joe, Rod, Buzz, Jimmy, John & Carmen.

The Vella's: Ed, John, Carmen, Tony, Larry, David & Andreanna.

23 of Nanna's grandkids. Back row: Dominic Suchyta, Steven and John Xuereb, Tony, and Fr. Ed Vella. Third row: Jeff and Tony Stone, Joseph Suchyta, John Stone. Second row: Rod, Tony (Buzz), Jimmy and Joe Xuereb, David Vella, Chris Suchyta, Larry behind John Vella. Front row: Carmen and Suzanne Xuereb, Carmen Vella, Ana Victoria Campos, Maria Suchyta, and Andreanna Vella.

NATIONAL GUARD AND BOY SCOUTS

Just a few years after arriving in the States, my brother Joe found himself volunteering in the National Guard for two years. He would go on weekend-long service to Grayling, MI, once or twice a month. This carried over through his marriage to Ginger McIntyre. They were married on Sept. 25, 1954.

While on duty, Joe met Stephen St. Angelo, who married Ida Aiello on August 28, 1954, just weeks before Joe and Ginger married. Joe and Steve became lifelong friends. Steve and Ida stood up at Joe and Ginger's wedding. Steven was even the best man. Brother Joe loved life, and he enjoyed his friends and family of six, five boys and a girl. You could be sure he would be there for you once he got to know you.

My brother Victor wanted to join the Boy Scouts, but Joe was totally against it. He assured my mom that if Victor became a scout, this would almost guarantee being drafted into the army, which my mother wanted no part of. I fondly remember long weekends on Military Street where Joe and Ginger rented an upper apartment from my dad while they searched for a house they could call their own. Most of us would gather at Joe's for a night-long game of Monopoly, and we all loved that game. We would spend hours playing Monopoly, which took us long into the night. Joe and Ginger finally found a home they liked on Wesson Street, about a mile away, but once again, my dad did not approve and had a problem with it. Joe went ahead and purchased it anyway. Perhaps my dad felt he could keep him under his rein if Joe was still renting from him.

Joe at Grayling, Michigan

VICTOR AND THE FRANCISCAN ORDER

Victor had wanted to be part of the Franciscan Order ever since he saw and heard a Franciscan priest begging in Malta. Franciscan priests would make their rounds to the neighboring farms and ask for donations. He asked Mother for a chicken, but she quickly announced that she couldn't do that as she still had young children to feed. Mother did offer him a dozen eggs as an alternative, and he politely accepted. Victor admired this particular friar's respectful, soft-spoken demeanor towards Mother. This stuck in his mind for many years to come. Leaving Malta as a young child of eleven, that incident would play a significant role in his life. Drawing back to that particular afternoon in Malta, Victor often thought of becoming a Franciscan like the one he had admired years prior. My mother eventually allowed him to enter the order when he was seventeen years of age. Her hesitation and reluctance before that were that she thought he was much too young and had his whole life ahead of him. When it was finally time for Victor to take his vows in Cincinnati, Ohio, we all piled into a couple of cars and drove as a caravan to be part of this joyful ceremony. Joe, leading the way,

Bro. Antonio Xuereb (Victor), Franciscan Friar, in the back stood Dad and brother-in-law Emanuel Vella.

happened to enter the wrong way into the grounds and proceeded to lead everyone up a steep hill. I'm sure we made quite the first impression and probably embarrassed Victor. Needless to say, we enjoyed the day and took several pictures.

Rena, Frank, Mother, Bro. Antonio Xuereb, Dad, Grace, Joe, and Dolores

The very next day, mother quickly took the rolls of films to Rose's Drug Store just around the corner on Campbell and Vernor. When it came time to pick up the developed photos, we were surprised to find that there were probably ten copies of each: small ones, very small ones, medium ones, and regular-size ones. Every developed photo had copies. Apparently, because of the language barrier, the druggist misunderstood my mother's instructions; unfortunately for us, we still had to pay the excessive development cost, but we had reminder photos everywhere around the house and in several of the China cabinet drawers for years to come.

Mother, Bro Antonio, Frank, Rena, Roddy and Dolores

Mother, Bro. Antonio, Frank.

Zija Sr. Carmen, Victor, and cousin Teresa in Malta.

Brother Antonio Xuereb.

Mother, Frank, Dad, and Victor.

SR. CARMELA XUEREB RSCJ

As I mentioned, Dad came from a family of seven children. Dad's youngest sister Carmela, better known as Sr. Carmen or Sr. Carmela RSCJ, came to visit us in Detroit in 1976. The habits nuns wore were being phased out, but Sr. Carmen still wasn't comfortable with removing her veil. When the realization hit that it was her hair that she was uncomfortable with, I took Sr. Carmela to the JC Penney's Salon. The hairdresser explained what she would do, and Sr. Carmen agreed to the haircut, after which she felt free and only wore a chapel veil. Mother kept Sr. Carmela's long salt and pepper-colored braids. They immediately held a spot in her China cabinet for years. We had a wonderful three weeks with Zija Carmen. She got to know her brother John and his family and cousins, and she also met her brother Emmanuel after years of absence. I was able to get a photo of the three: Ziju Leli, meaning Uncle Emmanuel, who left Malta in 1930 at the age of 22. He was a very shy man who never married and lived alone for years. He kept putting his hands up, not wanting to take a picture. He, too, retired from Ford Motor Co. Dad would see him now and then and, later in life, convinced him to come and be a caretaker at one of his properties and later offered him a place just next door to us, in Marija's house. He was very happy

Joe Shuereb, Sr. Carmen & Dad.

living next door to us. Mother made many dinners for him. We came over often, and if he was visiting, we'd announce ZIJU in a loud voice, and he would laugh and cover his face. We corresponded with Sr. Carmela for years, and I always admired her beautiful penmanship. Sr. Carmela passed away in Malta on February 21st, 1986, at 70 years of age.

Note: Ziju Emmanuel passed away at the Veteran's Hospital in Allen Park on the 17th of December 1984. Ziju served our country from Sept. 1942 - Sept. 1945 in the U.S. Army.

Ziju Emmanuel Xuereb.

Sr. Carmen with Andreanna Vella & Ziju Emmanuel..

Sr. Carmen arriving in Detroit.

Sr. with Joe & Dominic.

THE FENECH FAMILY

On Dragoon Street lived my dad's longtime friend, Gamri [John Mary] Fenech. They were together every spare minute; their friendship goes back to Mosta, Malta. Perhaps Dad and John Fenech were related as Dad's grandmother in the 1800s was Grazia Fenech. I think my dad wanted to move to Dragoon Street because across the street, at 1536 Dragoon, his best friend lived. Gamri and Josephine had three sons, Sam, Emmanuel, and Joe. Emmanuel, the middle son, was killed during the Vietnam War, which was an awful time for everyone; he was only 21 years of age when he was killed. My sister Dolores recalls our dad being the first one to drop what he was doing to comfort his friend. Their younger son Joe was born late in life for Josephine, and she would always make jokes about it. When Mrs. Fenech laughed, her whole body would jiggle; her laughter was so full of life that it was contagious.

Gamri was one of the few Maltese men that I knew who didn't work at Ford Motor Co. or General Motors; he worked for Parke-Davis and Company Pharmaceutical Plant. My dad was beside himself when his best friend died at 62 years of age; he lost a piece of himself that day in 1976. Josephine, his wife, was much younger than him, and she died at 63 years of age on July 25th of 1986. This family did not live long lives; even the boys died much too soon.

John 4/22/14 – 7/4/76
Josephine 11/3/22 - 7/25/86
Manuel 12/6/45 - 4/26/67
Joe 5/5/57 - 6/16/15
Sam 9/8/44 - 9/23/21

John and Josephine Fenech.    *Josephine Xuereb and Josephine Fenech.*

Dad John Xuereb with his best friend John Fenech.

CONNIE ZERAFA

Connie was a gentle soul. A young, heavy-set lady in her 30s with a mental awareness level of a five- or six-year-old child. She lived with her elderly parents, just two blocks from us on Eldred and Campbell. Mr. Zerafa was the local shoemaker, the best around, who owned a small shop on Junction St. just a block or so away from home. Connie had an older brother who was a Roman Catholic priest; he died in a horrific car accident. Connie would make the daily rounds, visiting all the Maltese homes in the neighborhood, back then that covered several homes up and down Campbell St. and in between. She would casually walk into your home unannounced in her heavy black shoes, dragging her one bad foot as she added a twist to it while she headed for the kitchen and sat. She would always laugh and smile; her conversation was very limited to none, mostly consisting of laughter. The Maltese homemakers, such as my mother, would make her a cup of tea and offer her cookies. My mother usually sat with her and made her feel at home while she made small talk with her and asked how her mom and dad were. She would sit awhile, enjoy her tea and biscuits and hospitality, and then head off to another house to repeat the same. Her mother often called the ladies and asked that they not feed her as she was gaining weight, but no one could say no to Connie; besides, she would sit until she got her tea and cookies. Everyone enjoyed her company; she was never a bother, just an innocent soul out making the neighborhood rounds. You could expect her like clockwork; she had the Maltese homes mapped out, and it would take her from lunch until dinner to visit with everyone. Thinking back now, I couldn't imagine something like this happening with everyone's busy schedule and the uncertainty on the streets; life was simpler and safer, I would venture to say, back in the '50s and '60s. I don't recall how Connie passed.

Connie Zerafa Oct 20, 1928 - March 1975 (age 46)

THE NEIGHBORS

The Fitzpatrick/Perez family was the greatest Irish/Spanish neighbors, and all our neighbors around us were wonderful. The Fernandez family across the street, the Jolly family next to the abandoned house, Mrs. Stitsman who lived further down, Tom and Mary Nall who lived next to the Fitzpatrick's, and many more. I credit this to being a small, close-knit city block. Mr. John Fitzpatrick was a Michigan State Representative, and I clearly remember that every election season, he would gather all the children in the neighborhood to help distribute flyers with information and his picture on them. We would be assigned a neighborhood precinct, usually around a school, where we stood and handed a flyer to every voter entering the building and asked for their vote. Thinking back, I wish I had saved a flyer or two over these years. Even though we were young kids, we took our job seriously. We were so proud to be part of the team. When the votes were tallied, and Mr. Fitzpatrick won, we felt we had helped and done our part. We were each rewarded with praise and two dollars for our hard work, which was a lot of money back then, especially for young kids like us.

Mom & Dad on the new porch with Mrs. Perez next door. Tom & Mary Nall at next house.

Dad, Mrs. Eva Fitzpatrick & Rena. John J. Fitzpatrick(75) passed on Jan. 10, 1986.

Carmena, husband Frank Fernandez Medo and his mother Shirley Fernandez.

DAD'S MIDLIFE CRISIS

Although my dad worked at Ford Motor Co., he loved his Chrysler-Plymouth and General Motors Buick automobiles. His very first car in the States was a 1950 Plymouth (pictured here). Not only did he arrive in Detroit in August of 1950, but he also managed to purchase a car and, later, a house before his family followed just ten months later, in June of 1951. He had other cars over the years, like a 1956 Mercury Bel Air, but I distinctly remember my dad coming home with a 1964 Oldsmobile, a burgundy convertible with a white top and white leather interior seats. He was 54 years old, and the first thing that came out of mother's mouth was, "What, you think you're 20 or something?" My mother never accompanied my dad when it came time to pick out cars or homes.

Dolores on the hood of a 1951 Mercury.

Dolores, Rena & Dad with his 1956 Mercury Bel Air

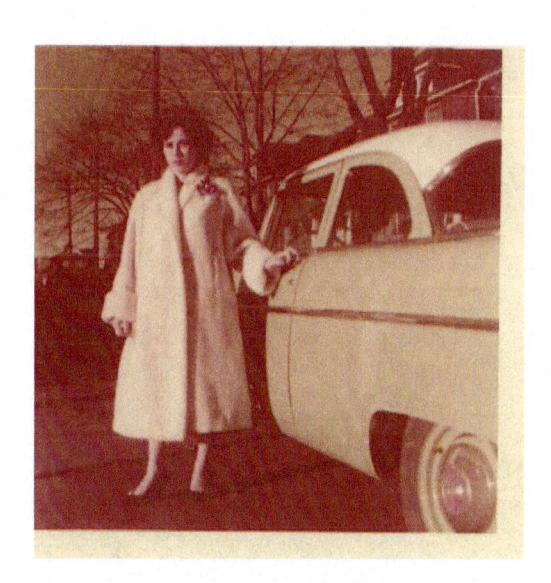

Grace, always styling.

Dad with grandson Ed Vella.

171

Dolores accompanying Grace and Manuel during a date.

YEAR 1968

This was the year the three youngest Xuereb siblings were married within five months of each other. Dolores is in May, Rena in June, and Frank is in October. I don't believe mother ever got over the fact that she had no children left in the house. It was devastating, to say the least. After all, she's been a mom since 1930, which is thirty-eight years with children around her.

✠✠✠✠✠

The Maltese were slowly starting to leave the Southwest Redeemer area and move to Dearborn and Dearborn Heights. My dad spotted a three-bedroom house in Dearborn Heights that he liked and took mother to see. This was the very first time my dad included my mom in a decision. Perhaps he knew she would never move. Mother started to cry and said, "Now? I don't need this big house now; everyone is gone." Dad never made any more mention of moving; they lived out their remaining years at 5840 Baker St.

Mother's seven children decided to present her with a mother's ring one Mother's Day. Dad jumped in and put the ring on her finger like he was the one who came up with the idea. That was Dad being a prankster once again.

Dad pretending that he can read, proudly holds up the newspaper.

DEPARTMENT OF IMMIGRATION

In 1995, we received a letter from the Department of Immigration and Naturalization that Mother had to update her immigration card by a certain date or she would face deportation. Many people paid no attention to such a letter, but we abided and certainly didn't want our mother to be sent back to Malta after 44 years. I took her to the nearest office on Jefferson Ave. in Detroit. We waited in line and had to venture across the street for passport pictures. Let me emphasize the right ear had to be showing, so the regular passport photos we brought were not accepted. Two months later, she received her new immigration card.

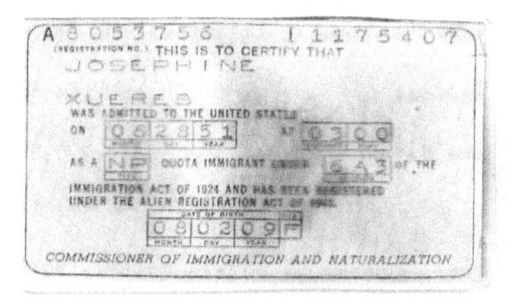

Mother's original immigration card, front and back.

Mother's new immigration card, front, and back.

MOTHER'S LAST TRIP TO MALTA

In May of 1995, when my mother was nearing the age of 86, my husband, Fernando Campos, convinced her and graciously escorted her to Malta for a final visit. While we were visiting the old farm in Qawra, where she grew up, she spelled out exactly how she and her sister would sneak out and walk down to the sea in the area called "Tal-Melħ." My niece Doris Gatt Scicluna was amazed at how much my mother could recall the "old days," but the fact is she was experiencing the onset of dementia, which has a great memory bank of the past and very poor retention of the present. During her final three weeks in Malta, she did exceptionally well, and I'm so grateful to my husband, Fernando, for suggesting and convincing my mother to take a trip to see her daughter and her family. He kept telling her, "Nanna, do you want to go to Malta." She thought he was joking and would laugh and say, "Oh come ONNNN." He'd reply, "No nanna, I'm serious. I'll take you." I said, "Mother, don't you want to pick the huge lemons at your mom's farm?" (Now, these lemon trees would probably be a hundred or more years old by now.) She gave it a lot of thought, and sure enough, when I went over the following day, she had already started packing. I'm so appreciative of the opportunity to accompany her one last time so she could have what turned out to be her last visit with her eldest daughter and her family. She would never complain but would tell me that Marija would never come to America, so I had to go there to see her. And I know she was glad she did, and I know Marija and her family were so happy to have her there for three weeks. She did exceptionally well during the flight; when we arrived, she didn't want the wheelchair provided, saying everyone would think she was old. I told her you'll be fine. My sister and her whole family, plus my cousin Francis and her husband Andrew were there to greet her. You could see the happiness on their faces. We had a memorable three weeks. We were there just after Mother's Day, but we had a beautiful celebration during this special time. We even welcomed our fifth generation, Michela Gatt, to our family. The departure was such a sad time, knowing this was her last trip.

Chris Gatt, his father Sam, his Mother Marija holding Michela and Nanna

COUSIN MARY AND CHARLIE

BUTTIGIEG

Mom and Dad had several nephews and nieces, especially in Malta and Australia, but also all over the states and Europe. The ones that stand out are Ziju Censu (Vincent), my dad's older brother's children. His son Joseph Xuereb (who changed his name to Shuereb, for clarity) left Malta when he was 21 years of age. Joe told me a few years back, just before he died in 2015, that as a seven-year-old child, he would look out to the sea and have visions of large ships on the horizon; he promised himself that he would one day be on one of those ships. He arrived in the States on March 29, 1948. He was joined by his uncle Joseph Sant, who sponsored him. Joe Shuereb went on to sponsor his siblings, Mary (22) and John (19), who came on the SS Brazil. They left Malta on July 5th, 1950, and arrived in the port of New York on July 20, 1950. John married Evelyn Debono, and they raised seven children and lived in Lincoln Park, where Evelyn still resides. Joe left us on January 11, 2015. Mary went on to marry Charlie Buttigieg. They also lived in Lincoln Park with two small daughters, Vicky and Theresa. They came over often to visit, and mother felt like a mom to her. Charlie also worked at Ford Motor Co., and during one difficult layoff period, he waited and waited to be called back to work, but he could not wait any longer. Since he had family in Australia, he made arrangements and packed up his family for a permanent move. Just then, he was called back to Ford Motor Co., but it was too late; all arrangements were in place. Mary was so sad to leave her brothers and our family. They had a difficult first few years in Australia, farming night and day, but they managed to buy some land that would be very fruitful for them in the end. They went on to add four more children to the family, and their immediate family grew as the children got older. Unfortunately, Mary was stricken with dementia, as her younger sister Angela was in Malta before her and most of the Xuereb women in our family; she passed away on August 16, 2011, and was born on August

8, 1928. Only after her husband Charlie passed before her on April 28, 2010, born on February 6, 1927. They made a point of visiting Michigan and Malta every two years, and we always enjoyed spending time with them. My only regret is not taking mother to visit her brothers in Australia. She had not seen them since they left Malta. It would have been nice for Mother to reconnect and have visited them as well.

L to R: Theresa, (Joe Xuereb's second wife), Grace, Angela Xuereb Fenech (visiting from Malta), sister of Joe Shuereb & John Xuereb, Mother, Evelyn, JoAnn & Joe Shuereb, Joe, Emanuel (Grace's husband), John Xuereb (Evelyn's husband) in the front, Fr. Edward Vella CssR (son of Grace & Emanuel).

Charlie Buttigieg & Wife Mary Xuereb Buttigieg (visiting from Australia), Mother, John & Evelyn Debono Xuereb, in the back Joe with 1st wife JoAnn Shuereb.

Marija Xuereb Gatt (John's daughter), Cousin Angela Xuereb Fenech (Censu's daughter), Cousin Sr. Mary Xuereb Rscj (Salvu's daughter), Mother and Cousin Sr. Josephine Xuereb Rscj (Also Salvu's Daughter).

Note: Sr. Mary Xuereb Rscj spent about 40 Years In Bangalore, India.

Sr. Carmela Xuereb RSCJ (aunt) and Sr. Josephine Xuereb RSCJ (cousin).

Marija with her sister-in-law Carmena Vassallo, and mother-in-law Marija Gatt.

Dolores Stone, Zija Sr. Carmela, Marija Gatt cousins Teresa & Sr. Josephine Xuereb

Note: In Malta, it is very common to name your home: notice "Detroit House" on the left.

Cousin Bertu and Maria Xuereb's family of 11 children and their families.

Dad's Zija Carmela Sant Gauci and her son cousin Monsignor Paul Gauci Monsignor, who moved to New Orleans to join his parents.

Cousin Angela Xuereb Fenech and family.

Dad and his friend Namru.

Karminu Xuereb, everyone called him Namru, died in Malta on March 17, 1997, at the age of 86. Namru lived in Detroit for several years and entertained us at several club functions, both at the Maltese American Clubs in Downtown Detroit and in Dearborn. He was a master at Qanni-style singing and had everyone in stitches.

From left to right:-
my daughter Gracie
Mrs. Carmena Gauci (my brother wife Salvu)
Mr. Salvu Gauci (my brother)
Joe and Charlie (my brother children)
my daughter Mary (Bride) & her husband
Mr. & Mrs Gauci (my brother Paul & his wife)
Mrs. Carmena Vella
Miss Rose Gauci (Mr. Mrs. Paul daughter)

My dad's cousins were at Mary and Leli Vella's wedding. I grew up hearing their names.

Fr. Ed. Vella C.Ss.R during his ordination in Chicago, Illinois. Back row: John & Jeff Stone. Frank & Gail Xuereb, Stoney Stone. Next row: Joe Suchyta, Andreanna Vella, Rita Vell, Sally & Tony Vella. Middle row: John Vella, hiding is Mary Vella, Pat Vella, Dolores Stone, Suzanne Xuereb, Rena Xuereb, and Steven Xuereb. Next row: Theresa & Joe Xuereb, Emanuel & Grace Vella with son Fr. Ed Vella, Carmen Vella, Nanna Josephine. Front row: Tony Stone, Dominic & Chris Suchyta.

MOTHER IN LAS VEGAS

Earlier, I told you how Mother loved her numbers. Another great example is her trip to Las Vegas with my brother Joe, who was quite the regular there. During this one particular trip, he asked my mother to join him, which she did. They had a nice flight there and a nice suite waiting for them at the Bally's Hotel. When it came time to introduce her to the slot machines, my mother wanted to observe and study all her choices, and then, after careful consideration, she picked out the slot machine she would adopt. She got comfortable in the chair in front of the slot machine, pulled out her good luck charms from bingo, took out a small notebook, and proceeded to write. Let me explain her strategy. Before depositing money into the slot machine, she would log it into her notebook. Then, she would pull the handle and write down the results. If that pull gave her 0, she wrote it down; if it gave her anything else, she would also note it. Joe watched her for a while, almost laughing at her technique. Something was working for her, though. Perhaps it was beginner's luck, or perhaps it was her lucky charms, but she made out pretty good on that trip.

MOTHER'S PETS

While growing up on Baker Street, I always remember my mother having either a pet dog or cat and certainly birds, parrots, or canaries. I always remember how Nanna picked a certain ground weed from the yard (purslane) and put it in the bird cage that was usually in the kitchen and how the birds loved that weed. She generally had small dogs, except for the time my dad brought Princess home; she was a beautiful sandy-color Collie but not my mother's choice, so Princess had to stay outdoors and in the garage. My dad obtained this Collie from the owner of the hardware store on Vernor Highway, just around the corner from Baker Street, where we lived. There used to be a row of old wooden stores where the Spartan store, formerly A&P, now sits, and the hardware store that my dad often frequented sat in the middle. I also remember a cat named Mixi; my mom liked that name since this calico cat had a coat in three colors. I believe my mother was partial to cats the most, but I especially remember Penny, the small black and white mixed house dog my mom had. I felt she was more my pet than anyone else in the household.

I was around eleven and loved to carry her for a "walk" around the block. You see, she had great posture and could sit straight up on her hind legs while in my arms. I enjoyed the stares I got from my friends and strangers when they thought Penny was a circus dog doing tricks.

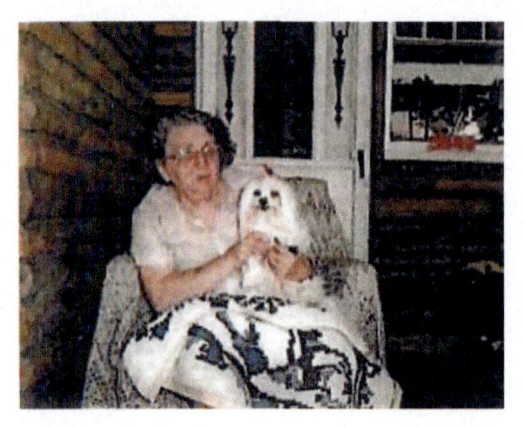

I remember one white Maltese dog we purchased for Mother for her 78th birthday. Tai was his name, and he was a show dog with purebred papers, complete with a family history line. I remember spending a few hundred dollars for that dog. We thought Tai would be a great companion for Mother, but the fact was, Mother didn't care for male dogs (something we quickly learned) and they never bonded. My son Chris was in his first year of high school at Cass Tech High School, and since he was home during the two-week teacher strike, Tai grew close to Chris. Maltese dogs are known to be faithful to one person.

Her last dog on Baker St. was Toby. There were more pets in between, but these I especially remember. A year or so earlier, I decided with my children to leave our home, which was just a mile away, and move in with Mother. She was trying so hard to live alone but having an awful time with it and, especially during the night; I couldn't blame her. This fear worsened after she was broken into and tied up, as I spelled out earlier. I would get a daily evening call from Mother asking for one of the kids to come to spend the night with her.

I love my mom and would do anything for her, but this was getting old after a few months and was not fair to my kids, especially during Christmas break, so we decided to occupy the upstairs flat on Baker St. and extra bedrooms downstairs. This worked out fine for the kids since Holy Redeemer School was just down the street, and I could walk to work at the High School Alumni Office. Everything was going well until she started to complain about my three boys being loud or playing outside. She would often take a broom handle and hit the room ceiling when the boys were too loud for her. I had to constantly explain to Mother that we were there for her, not because we needed a place to stay. We had a home sitting empty.

She would apologize and state, "You know how young boys make me crazy."

✠✠✠✠✠

One memory my son Chris recalls while spending nights at Nanna's is her always opening the house door that led into the hallway where the basement door was. Late each evening just past midnight, after faithfully watching The Johnny Carson Show, Nanna would open this door and in a deep voice, would announce, "Toby GO-O-O-O". Her small dog Toby would immediately move slowly out the door and into the basement with her tail between her legs and head and ears down. You had to witness this to appreciate it. Neither dogs nor cats were ever allowed to stay in the living quarters of the house for their nightly sleep.

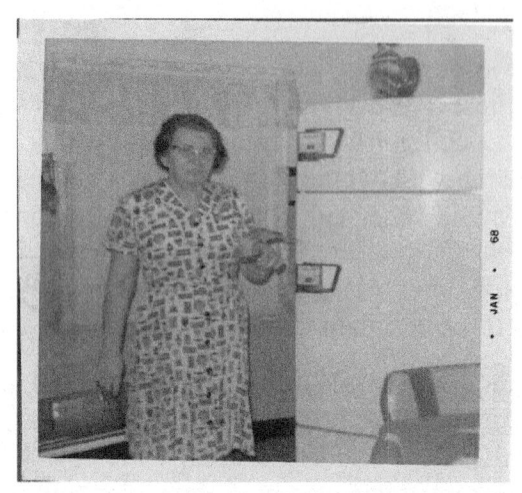

Mother and her parrot

Rena with our dog Penny

HOLY REDEEMER AND FRIENDS

After my father's death in January of 1980, my mother tried so hard to be independent. She took herself to Dr. Kuhn's office just across the street from Holy Redeemer Church on Junction St., conveniently two blocks from our house on Baker St. She would go to the bank, right next to the doctor's office, pay her bills. She would walk to the dime store, S.S. Kresge, located across from the church and down half a block on Vernor Highway, where she would always buy something. It was considered rude to go into a store and not make even a small purchase. Then, she would attend the daily 11:15 a.m. mass at Holy Redeemer Church. She eventually made friends with the Maltese posse, who also attended daily mass. There was Mr. Galea, who lived on the other side of Vernor, the lone male among ladies like Mrs. Vassallo, who walked the mile hike or took the bus, Mrs. Anne Mifsud, who lived down the street from us, and a few others who, sorry to say, I don't recall their names. They all had their favorite individual pews in church, almost like they were reserved for them. In fact, at Mother's funeral, my daughter Maria placed a bouquet of flowers on HER seat in her honor.

The Maltese posse invited mother to their routine of McDonald's on Vernor just another city block, the opposite direction from her house. There, they would enjoy lunch while talking about Malta and old times. I sometimes joined them with my young daughter Ana Victoria. I would just listen to the stories of Malta as each took turns talking about their village. Mother always bought a fish sandwich and coffee; she would always dunk her sandwich in her coffee, something Ana Victoria never understood; but I told her Nanna was having problems with her dentures, she still didn't understand. From McDonald's, the posse would go their separate ways, but not before they synchronized their agenda; who was returning for Novena on Tuesday evenings or who was going to bingo on Wednesday evenings in the Blue Room at Holy Redeemer, etc. All I know is that mother looked forward to her daily routine with her church friends, another good reason to have lived on Baker Street, and it made her alone years a little more acceptable.

While working at Holy Redeemer High School Alumni office, the posse would pass my office window, the same window sill that my dad, 13 years prior, would trustingly leave his cigar butt every Sunday when he went to noon mass. I watched these ladies and Mr. Galea meet up while walking into church and then again as they left and waved to me. Over the years, with death slowly consuming the group one by one, they went from an average of seven strong down to only one, that being my mother. It was so sad to watch her walk towards the church alone and then later walk towards me, waving as she headed to McDonald's.

1993 Anne Mifsud (90), Mother (84).
Photo courtesy of Dolores Stone.

DAD'S DEATH

My dad had a few heart attacks and strokes, but they were getting harder and harder to repair. One stroke left him with a limp, and he had to use a cane, but do you think that stopped him? He carried on as usual, driving everywhere and going from house to house, trying to make any repairs himself. I had to go along with him to help a few times. He continued to enjoy his pastime at the race track. He once took my daughter Maria, who was 13 at the time, to the Windsor Race track. There he proceeded to tell Maria that this was where he wanted to die. Maria was shocked but just thought Dad was talking out loud again. Three weeks later, my mom got a phone call to have someone call this number; she called my brother Joe, who made the phone call and was informed that our dad had just passed away at the Windsor race track. Joe, along with his son Roddy, made the trip over to Windsor to identify him, make funeral arrangements, and bring back his car. My dad got excited when the horse he bet on was coming in first and suffered a heart attack or a stroke. His pack of cigarettes was right next to him, with his dollar still in the sleeve for the return home on the bridge. My dad made a large tuna fish salad before he left and told my mom he would eat it on his return. That salad sat in the refrigerator for days and days. Mother blamed herself for not going with my dad as she usually did. My dad was only 69 years of age when he passed on January 18, 1980. Ironically, my sister-in-law Gail Xuereb, Frank's wife, also died at 69 years of age and also on January 18th, 20 years later.

BACK IN NEW YORK

My son Joseph Suchyta once gave me a very special Christmas gift: a plaque from Ellis Island. He had my family added to The American Immigrant Wall of Honor at Ellis Island. Even though we did not step foot on Ellis Island, they allowed us to be on their wall. I went back to New York, and while on the ferry to Ellis Island, as we reached closer and closer to the symbolic Statue of Liberty, I wondered, as I gazed at her, what if anything, my mother was thinking and feeling as she drew closer; was she relieved? Was she sad? What exactly was she feeling? After spending a great deal of time observing the magnificent building, which held years of stories, photos, and history, I went outside to find and witness the Xuereb Family on the wall. I searched and searched every part of the wall that wrapped all around the back of the complex, and I found a few Xuereb names but no one I recognized; I was starting to give up, thinking maybe it was not done yet, but Joe assured me he saw it online so I kept looking, and sure enough, it was the last set of walls. It was so special that we were the only ones under the X, like it was all ours. My hair was standing up when I locked my eyes on our family name; I was so proud of the courage it took my parents to eventually get to this new land.

IN CONCLUSION

I don't believe my siblings nor I ever thought of ourselves as immigrants while growing up, especially since so many of our friends and classmates came over from Malta as we did, some before us and several after us. Many of our friends came from other parts of the world as well, or their parents or grandparents did. The Xuereb family lived in a pretty diversified neighborhood in Southwest Detroit. As I said previously, we never gave the idea of our family being immigrants much thought. Even when we all became U.S. citizens, then married and started raising children.

I think it finally sank in for me when I turned 42, the age my mother Josephine left Malta, and my first-born daughter Maria was just 20 years of age, nearly the same age as my oldest sister Marija was when we left her behind with her young family. I truly feel that is when it hit me. On several occasions, I would sit and go over the whole thought process of leaving my family and friends, especially leaving my daughter behind, and what strength and courage that must have taken for Josephine, our mother, the family monarch. People who have never experienced the gut-wrenching agony of separation from home and family and everything that goes with it will never understand the pain and anguish it takes to leave behind one's land of birth. Most likely, Josephine's mind was swamped with memories of childhood, adolescence, and familiar times and faces. William Shakespeare was indeed correct in noting that parting is such sweet sorrow. Ahead was a future of uncertain promise in uncertain lands populated by uncertain people whose habits, mannerisms, and emotions were foreign to our Maltese culture.

✠✠✠✠✠

Thinking about this whole ordeal as often as I have brought me to the conclusion that we are as much Maltese today as we were the day we waved our loved ones a final farewell at the Grand Harbour. Our

American nationality in no way changes our desire and pride to remain Maltese. Nobody, not even people of our kind, who may not understand the anguish of divided loyalties, has a right to or can rob us of our heritage. We shall always remain sons and daughters of our beloved island in the sun. They often say that over time, you become a clone of your parents. I can somewhat see this in myself and catch myself sounding, acting, and making the same expressions my dear Mother often made.

One thing I will never inherit from my mother is her courage. The strength to leave Malta, the only home she had ever known all her life, and venture onto a new and foreign land, not speaking the language and with six children in hand from ages nineteen to four, and more importantly, leaving behind her firstborn and her young family thinking she would never see them again. I'm sorry, but this would take more strength than I could muster, and to this day, I don't know where my mother found her courage. Some nights when I start missing my mother more than usual, I make myself a cup of Maltese tea with a splash of Carnation Evaporated milk, then I slip into the purple chenille bathrobe I bought for her years ago and wrap myself in her memory. Somehow, I feel a little more secure, warm, and closer to her when I have her well-worn robe close to my body. I think of how she loved that robe after a bath, especially during the cold winter months. Then I would get a chuckle when I started to think of my dad coming out of the bathroom after a bath with his wild, uncombed hair and wearing my mother's bulky yellow, Terry cloth bathrobe from years earlier.

At first, it was one of his customary jokes, but then he realized it really was warm and would always make use of it after a bath. I, on the other hand, never thought of purchasing a men's bathrobe for him to enjoy. I don't think that notion was popular back in the late '60s – '70s.

During the process of gathering and writing, I thought of all the questions I should have asked my mom and dad. Now, the answers seem to be lost forever, but hopefully, with the help of family and friends, the information and stories we were able to resurrect will live on, be absorbed, and be passed on for others to enjoy. I pray that my mother's angelic wings will always be wrapped around us and keep us safe.

John and Josephine Xuereb are buried at St. Hedwig Cemetery in Dearborn Heights, Michigan.

MAY THEY REST IN PEACE.

My Mother

My mother is a woman like no other. She gave me life, nurtured me, taught me, dressed me, fought for me, held me, shouted at me, kissed me, but most importantly loved me unconditionally.

There are not enough words I can say to describe just how important my mother was to me, and what a powerful influence she continues to be..

Mother, I Love You.

IN MEMORY

Josephine Gauci Xuereb (August 2, 1909 - January 6, 2003)

Vittorja Xuereb (March 19, 1939 - March 19, 1939) 4th child of John/Josephine Xuereb

Josephine Vella (December 25, 1960 - December 25, 1960) 4th child of Grace/Manuel Vella

Catherine Ann Vella (June 7, 1963 - January 7, 1970) 6th child of Grace/Manuel Vella

John Paul Xuereb (August 6, 1910 - January 18, 1980)

Catrina Brincat (March 16, 2005 - February 24, 2008) 2nd child of Claudine Gatt/Chris Brincat

Marija Xuereb Gatt (August 24, 1930 - March 13, 2010) 1st child of John/Josephine Xuereb

Joseph Xuereb (April 23, 1936 - March 20, 2010) 3rd child of John/Josephine Xuereb

Joseph Gatt (September 3, 1928 - July 11, 2012), husband of Marija Xuereb Gatt

Gail Marie Grand Xuereb (September 23, 1943 - January 18, 2013), wife of Frank Xuereb

Grace Xuereb Vella (December 10, 1931 - May 27, 2013) 2nd, child of John/Josephine

Emanuel Vella (December 9, 1932 – July 7, 2017), husband of Grace Xuereb Vella

Frank Xuereb (August 10, 1942 - December 26, 2020), 5th child of John/Josephine Xuereb

Harliss (Stoney) Stone (October 7, 1944 - October 1, 2021), husband of Dolores Xuereb Stone

Virginia (Ginger) McIntyre Xuereb (August 5, 1936 - May 5, 2022) 1st wife of Joseph Xuereb

Theresa Atkinson Xuereb (April 18, 1941 - May 12, 2022) 2nd, wife of Joseph Xuereb

There are things that we don't want to happen but have to accept, things we don't want to know but have to learn, and people we can't live without have to let go.

~Author Unknown

MALTESE RECIPES

ALJOTTA (FISH SOUP)

Ingredients

1 tsp. tomato paste
2 tbsp. olive oil
1 bay leaf
1 onion, diced
Fresh mint
1 clove of garlic, chopped
8 cups water
6 tomatoes, sliced
3.5 oz. rice
1.75 pounds; cod, halibut, flounder or snapper, cleaned and cut into 4 pieces.
Salt, and pepper
2 lemons (1 for juice, 1 for garnish)
Frozen pieces are good too.
Fresh parsley

INSTRUCTIONS

1. In a large pot, sauté the onion and garlic in olive oil until soft and golden.
2. Add the tomatoes, tomato paste, bay leaf, mint, and water.
3. Bring the mixture to a boil, then add the fish.
4. Reduce the heat and simmer until the fish meat is white and soft.
5. Remove the fish from the soup, allow it to cool until you can handle it, then remove the head, tail, skin, and bones. I prefer to use frozen cod.
6. Strain the soup broth and return it to the pot.
7. Cook the rice in the soup broth by bringing it to a boil and cooking until the rice is tender.
8. Return fish meat to the pot. Season with salt, pepper, and a squeeze of lemon.
9. Serve hot with lemon wedges and parsley as garnish.

BIGILLA (BROAD BEAN DIP)

Ingredients

1 lb. dried broad beans
2 tsp. chopped parsley
1 garlic crushed
1 chili pepper
a dash of hot sauce
1 tbsp. fresh mint, finely chopped
2 tbsp. olive oil

Instructions

1. Soak beans overnight and replace the water a few times.
2. Add salt to taste, boil, and simmer until the beans are soft.
3. Mash beans, add all other ingredients and place them in a serving dish.
4. Add olive oil on top.

Serve hot or cold.

BRAGIOLI (STUFFED BUNDLE OF BEEF)

Ingredients

4 slices lean beef
mixed spice
small can 3 oz. tomato paste
tsp. dried basil
4 slices of chopped bacon
5 oz. onions
chopped parsley
14 oz. tomatoes
salt and pepper
breadcrumbs
2 hardboiled eggs cut into small pieces
olive oil
7 oz. peas
water

Instructions

1. Prepare the beef by flatting them on a board.
2. In a bowl, mix the chopped bacon, chopped eggs, parsley, salt, 60wpepper, and a little bread crumbs.
3. With a tablespoon, fill 4 flatting beef, then roll them up and put toothpicks so the filling won't come out.
4. Put the 4 wrapped beef pieces in a deep-frying pan with some oil. Fry the beef rolls slightly just to seal. Set it aside.
5. Fry the onions in the hot olive oil do not brown, add the spice, basil, tomato paste, and chopped tomatoes.
6. Pour the tomato mixture on the beef rolls, cover with water or beef stock, bring to a boil, and simmer for 20 mins.
7. Add the peas and continue simmering for another hour on a very low flame till thick.
8. Serve with boiled Potatoes.

BRUNGIEL MIMLI (STUFFED EGGPLANT)

Ingredients

4 large eggplants
1 tomato, chopped
1 lb. ground meat (beef & pork)
2 oz. bread crumbs
2 tbsp. margarine
1 onion, sliced
2 eggs, beaten
3 garlic cloves, crushed
1 tbsp. parsley chopped
4 oz. grated parmesan cheese
2 tsp. tomato paste
salt and pepper to taste

Instructions

1. Cut each eggplant in half lengthwise. Parboil halves for 10 minutes.
2. Scoop out the middle and save.
3. Fry onion and garlic.
4. Add tomato paste, meat, eggplant pulp, tomato, parsley, and bread crumbs.
5. Cook until meat is done, stirring well.
6. Remove from heat.
7. Add the beaten eggs, cheese, salt, and pepper.
8. Use this mixture to stuff halved eggplants.
9. Sprinkle the tops with breadcrumbs & cheese.
10. Bake in a 350F oven for about an hour.

FROGA TAT-TARJA (PASTA OMELET)

Ingredients

10 ½ oz. Vermicelli pasta
3 eggs
2 tbsp. chopped parsley
3 oz. Parmesan cheese
Salt & pepper
olive oil

Instructions

1. In a large pot, cook the pasta until al dente, strain, and set aside.
2. In a large bowl beat the eggs and mix all the ingredients, except the olive oil.
3. Add the cooked pasta and mix well.
4. Heat some olive oil in a large frying pan on medium heat. Add half of the pasta and egg until the mixture covers the bottom of the frying pan.
5. Let it cook until it turns golden, and flip it by placing a plate over the omelet and flip the omelet onto the plate. Add some more oil to the pan.
6. Slowly put the omelet back into the pan slowly and cook the other side.
7. Repeat with the remaining mixture.

GBEJNIET (FRESH MALTESE CHEESE)

Ingredients

1 gallon whole milk
3 tsp Rennet powder
3 tbsp. water
Salt
15 Cheese baskets (qwieleb)
Thermometer
Large pot to warm milk
Tray or dish to store cheese in baskets (a dripping tray is ideal)
Cloth to strain the ricotta from the whey and a strainer

Instructions

1. Place milk in large pot on a stove and gently warm.
2. Use a thermometer to check when the temperature of the milk reaches 100 degrees Fahrenheit. (Or warm to the touch, do not boil).
3. Remove off heat.
4. In a small cup place rennet powder and about 3 tbsp. water. Mix quickly and gently until dissolved, stir into milk.
5. Leave in kitchen on a table for 3 hours.
6. After 1.5 hours gently cut into the coagulating milk in vertical lines and leave for a further 1.5 hours. This helps the separation of the curds and whey.
7. Once the 3 hours have been completed, get 1 basket and scoop up the curds to fill the basket. Place in tray.
8. Keep doing this until all baskets have been filled and placed in the tray.
9. Set in a dripping pot before placing in the fridge.
10. Sprinkle salt on top of the curds and place in the fridge. Leave overnight.
11. The following morning turn the cheese over and sprinkle with salt again. Keep in the fridge for another 12 hours.
12. Your fresh gbejniet should then be ready.

PASTIZZI DOUGH
(courtesy of Maltese American Community Club)

Ingredients

5 cup flour
2 cups cold water
1 dash salt
3 cups shortening (Crisco)

Instructions

1. Use an electric mixer with a dough hook attachment.
1. Mix four, water, and salt on medium-high speed for 15 minutes. The dough should feel moist and soft. Cover for 1 hour.
2. Cut about one-eighth of the dough ball; cover the remaining dough and refrigerate.
3. Roll the dough out on a cool, slightly greased table.
4. Pull and spread the dough a little at a time until the dough is very thin.
5. Spread a generous amount of shortening (Crisco) all over the top of the dough.
6. Start at one end of the dough and roll, pulling back and up as you roll.
7. Repeat this process with the remaining dough, rolling each layer inside the stretched dough until the roll is about 1 to 1 ½ inches thick.
8. Refrigerate until ready to use.
9. When ready to use, cut the dough roll into 1-inch sections.
10. Lay each section on its side so the circles face up.
11. Spread each circle carefully; don't work too much to approximately a 4-inch circle.
12. Add 1 tablespoon of filling (see below) on one side of the circle and fold the dough over.
13. Press the edges to seal. Place on a greased cookie sheet. Bake in a hot oven at 425F for 30 to 35 minutes until golden.

Continue >>

\>\> Continued

1. CHEESE FILLING
(courtesy of Maltese American Community Club)

Ingredients

1 lb. ricotta cheese
2 large eggs
1 pinch salt

Instructions

In a medium bowl, mix all three ingredients until well combined.

2. MEAT FILLING
(courtesy of Maltese American Community Club)

Ingredients

1 medium onion finely chopped
2 tsp. Olive oil
1 lb. lean ground beef
2 tsp. tomato paste
½ tsp. Italian spices
1 large can of peas, drained
salt and pepper to taste

Instructions

1. In a large skillet, cook onion in oil until softened.
2. Add beef and brown, stir in tomato paste and spices.
3. Stir in peas, salt, and pepper.
4. Cool completely.

Continue \>\>

>> Continued

3. PEA FILLING
(courtesy of Maltese American Community Club)

Ingredients

¾ cup dried green split peas
1 onion finely chopped
2 garlic cloves crushed
1 tbsp. olive oil
1 tbsp. mild curry powder
¼ cup cold water

Instructions

1. In a medium saucepan, cover peas with water; heat over high heat to boiling. Reduce heat to medium-low, simmer, uncovered, until the peas are cooked, then drain.
2. In a large skillet, cook onion and garlic in oil until translucent. Stir in curry powder; cook 30 seconds.
3. Add peas and cold water; cook until most liquid has evaporated, stirring frequently.
4. Cool completely.

4. CORNED BEEF FILLING
(courtesy of Maltese American Community Club)

Ingredients

3 tbsp. vegetable oil
4 large carrots, finely diced
1 large onion, finely diced
8 small potatoes, quartered
2 cans (12 oz.) corned beef
2 tbsp. tomato paste

Continue >>

>> **Continued**

Instructions

1. In a large skillet, heat the oil.
2. Add carrots and onions and cook until soft, adding a little water if necessary.
3. Boil potatoes, do not overcook.
4. When carrots are soft, stir in corned beef and tomato paste; cook until corned beef are broken down, and stir well.
5. Remove from heat. Mash the potatoes and stir into the corned beef mixture.
    Cool completely.

PIZZA TOAST

Ingredients

Bread Slices
Sliced Tomatoes
Shredded Mozzarella or Cheddar Cheese
Pepperoni/Sausage Slices (optional)
Salt and Pepper to Taste

Instructions

1. Preheat oven to 350F.
2. Butter the bread slices.
3. Cover with two or three thin slices of tomatoes. Season the tomatoes with pepper and salt and other herbs if you like.
4. If you prefer, add a couple of slices of pepperoni or sausage.
5. Spread the shredded cheese on the bread and place it on a baking sheet
6. Bake in a 350F hot oven until the cheese melts and the bread is slightly toasted.

RAVIOLI

Ingredients

<u>Dough</u>
7 oz. shifted flour
Pinch of salt
5 oz. semolina
2 beaten eggs

<u>Filling</u>
1 lb. ricotta
salt and pepper
2 eggs beaten
4 tbsp. grated parmesan cheese

Instructions

1. Start with the dough, and carefully mix sifted flour, semolina, and salt.
2. Add the eggs and knead until the dough is elastic, if to stiff, add a drop of cold water.
3. Rest for an hour while preparing the filling.
4. Put all the other ingredients, ricotta, beaten eggs, cheese, parsley, salt, and pepper into a Mixing bowl. Mix everything well.
5. Divide the dough into 4 pieces and roll it into long, thin strips. Dampen the edges with water.
6. Put small balls of ricotta about half an inch from the edge of the pastry and 1 inch apart.
7. Turn one edge of the pastry onto the other and press to seal.
8. Using a ravioli cutter, cut out the extra pastry about an inch away from the filling.
9. Let it rest for 10 minutes.
10. Boil in salted water till soft.
11. Serve with tomato sauce and grated cheese.

RICOTTA (WHEY CHEESE)

Ingredients

8 cups whole milk
1 ½ heavy cream
tsp. salt
¼ cup lemon juice

Instructions

1. Bring 8 cups of whole milk in a large pot over medium to high heat.
2. Add heavy cream and a tsp. of salt.
3. Bring to high heat for about 15 minutes, don't boil.
4. Add the lemon juice, stir, and turn off the heat. Let it sit for 5 minutes; don't stir.
5. Strain through a cheesecloth-lined strainer into a bowl.
6. Let it sit for 20 minutes or an hour, depending on how firm you want it to be.

ROSS IL-FORN (BAKED RICE)

Ingredients

2 cups rice in a pan, stir in 4 cups of water, allow to sit, and soak on the counter (do not cook)
1 lb. ground beef brown
half a chopped onion
Salt and pepper
6 oz can of tomato paste
1½ cups fresh grated cheese
4 beaten eggs

Instructions

1. Brown the ground beef with the onion, add salt and pepper.
2. Drain the rice mix well, and add to the beef mixture.
3. Add the tomato paste. Mix well.
4. Simmer for 20 minutes.
5. Grease a 2-quart baking dish and pour the mixture into it.
6. Add the cheese, then the eggs, and mix slightly. Add water if it looks dry.
7. Lightly add some more cheese on top of the mixture.
8. Bake in a 350F oven for about 45 minutes.
   20 minutes covered; 25 minutes uncovered.
9. Let cool, then cut into servings.

SOPPA TAL-ARMLA (WIDOW'S SOUP)

Ingredients

1 onion, diced
½ cauliflower, cut into bite-size pieces
3 to 4 cloves garlic, crushed
1 ½ tbsp. tomato paste
2/3 cup chopped parsley
2 celery stalks, sliced
2 potatoes, peeled and chopped
salt and pepper
2 carrots, peeled and chopped
vegetable or chicken stock enough to cover vegetable
1 kohlrabi, peeled and chopped
1 cup broad beans
6 gbejniet (Maltese cheese)

Instructions

1. Sauté garlic. Onion and parsley in butter and olive oil until soft.
2. Add potatoes, carrots, kohlrabi, broad beans, celery, peas, and cauliflower.
3. Add stock and tomato paste.
4. Stir well and season with salt and pepper.
5. Bring to a boil, cover, and simmer for about 15 to 20 minutes until vegetables are soft.
6. Garnish with parsley. Add one ġbejniet per person.

MINESTRA TAL-HAXIX (VEGETABLE SOUP)

Ingredients

4 beef neck bones or short ribs
2 turnips
4 potatoes
2 tomatoes
2 onions
2 carrots
1 lb. pumpkin
½ small can tomato paste
½ small cabbage
1 cup small shaped pasta
½ small cauliflower
5 cups of water

Instructions

1. Chop all the vegetables and place them in a pot.
2. Add 5 cups of water and tomato paste, and season.
3. Bring to a boil and let simmer until vegetables are tender.
4. Add a spoonful of olive oil.
5. Add pasta and simmer until done.

STUFFED TAL-FENEK (RABBIT STEW)

Ingredients

1 rabbit
1 cup peas
2 medium onions, sliced
Handful of dark raisins
6 garlic cloves, peeled
bouillon cubes
¼ Red Wine
2 bay leaves
3 large tomatoes, peeled and chopped
mixed herbs
2 tsp. tomato paste
1 tsp. olive oil
3 potatoes, peeled and quartered
salt and pepper
6 carrots peeled and sliced
flour

Instructions

1. Add salt and pepper to the flour. Mix well.
2. Roll rabbit portions in seasoned flour.
3. Cook rabbit in olive oil until slightly brown. Set aside.
4. Add onions, garlic, tomatoes, and potatoes to a large pot.
5. Add the fried rabbit.
6. Pour some of the wine over the ingredients. (My mom liked Morgan David).
7. Add tomato paste, bouillon cubes, and bay leaves.
8. Add peas and raisins.
9. Bring to a boil and simmer for about 1 1/2 hours.
10. Add more wine if the sauce begins to dry up.

TIMPANA (BAKED MACARONI PIE)

Ingredients

14oz. flaky dough
2 cups water or stock
2 lbs. macaroni
1 small finely chopped onion
1lb extra lean hamburger
salt and pepper
3 tbsp. tomato paste
14oz. grated Parmesan cheese
4 well-beaten eggs

Instructions

1. Preheat the oven to 375F.
2. In a large saucepan, cook the onion until tender.
3. Add the meat and brown for a couple of minutes.
4. Mix well with the tomato paste and two cups of water or stock.
5. Add salt and pepper to taste.
6. Cover the saucepan and let the sauce simmer for about twenty minutes.
7. Cook the macaroni in salted boiling water till tender, drain well, and place in a large mixing bowl.
8. Add the sauce, the Parmesan cheese, and the beaten eggs and mix well.
9. Grease a large baking dish with margarine.
10. Roll out the dough and line the dish with the dough.
11. Pour the pasta and sauce mixture into the baking dish.
12. Cover the top with the dough. Press the edges to seal the dish. With a fork, pierce the dough.
13. Brush with a beaten egg.
14. Bake for about one hour. The dough should turn golden brown.

NOTE: can also be made without the dough. Bake covered with foil for ½ hr., then uncovered for ½ hour till brown.

TORTA TAL-IRKOTTA (RIKOTTA PIE)

Ingredients

Pastry
1 ½ lbs. flour, shifted
4 ½ lbs. margarine
4 tbsp. olive oil
½ tsp. salt
enough water to bind

Filling
5 lbs. ricotta
salt and pepper
parsley
2 beaten eggs
3 tbsp. grated cheese
Chopped parsley

Instructions

1. Mix the pastry, cover it, and let it rest while you mix the filling.
2. Mix ricotta with eggs and work to a smooth mixture.
3. Add cheese, parsley, and seasoning. Check seasoning, important to get the right flavor.
4. Grease a pie pan, line it with pastry, and fill it with ricotta.
5. Egg wash the edges and cover with pastry.
6. Bake in a moderate oven until a nice golden brown.

TORTA TAL LAHAM (CORNED BEEF PIE)

Ingredients

6 sheets puff pastry
1 ½ lbs. pumpkin
2 onions
1 ½ lbs. potatoes
2 cans of corned beef
4 full Tbsp. basmati rice
3 Tbsp. tomato paste
1 ½ cups frozen peas
2 eggs
salt and pepper

Instructions

1. Preheat oven to 350F.
2. Spray and line a baking dish with puff pastry.
3. In a frying pan, fry the onion in a little oil. When soft, add tins of corned beef, soften it, and add tomato paste and eggs. Mix thoroughly and remove from heat after a minute.
4. Slice pumpkin and potato thinly.
5. Place sliced pumpkin and potato on a clean tea towel and dry off the extra moisture.
6. In a large mixing bowl, add corned beef mix, pumpkin and potato, raw rice, and cooked peas.
7. Season with salt and pepper and mix well.
8. Add pie filling to the pastry dish, cover it with sheets of pastry, and seal the sides well. Prick with a fork.
9. Brush with egg wash and bake in a preheated oven for about 1 ½ - 2 hours, till golden brown.

MALTESE SWEETS

BISKUTTINI TAL-LEWZ (ALMOND COOKIES)

(courtesy of Mary & Lewis Buhagiar)

Ingredients

I cup Almond Paste
1 large egg white
1 ¼ cup sugar
almond slivers
rice paper (optional)
line cookie sheet with parchment paper

Instructions

1. Preheat oven to 325F.
2. Work the almond paste into small pieces and place them into a mixer.
3. Add sugar and mix well.
4. Add the egg white and mix until moist and sticky (tacky). Approximately 2 minutes.
5. Drop by rounded tablespoons, 1 inch apart, onto rice paper (can be found at baking accessory stores, but not necessary).
6. Top with a sliver of almond. FYI: do not try to make them larger, as the paste will not fully cook inside.
7. Bake for 20 minutes on the middle shelf until golden brown.
8. When completely cool, carefully peel the cookies off the parchment paper. If you are using rice paper, merely cut between cookies. Makes approximately 18 cookies, which can be doubled to 36 cookies.

Continue >>

\>\> Continued

TO MAKE YOUR ALMOND PASTE:

Ingredients

1 ½ cups whole blanched almonds, toasted if desired.
1 ½ cups confectionary sugar.
1 large room-temperature egg white, more as needed, beaten slightly
¼ tsp. almond extract.

Instructions

1. Place the almonds and the confectionary sugar in the food processor and process to a meal-like consistency, scraping down the sides and over the bottom of the bowl often. Don't overprocess it. Should be crumbly.
2. Add the egg white and the almond extract. Process until it lumps together. If it remains crumbly, add more egg white, a few drops at a time.
3. Using a spatula, remove the almond paste from the food processor.
4. If not using it right away, place the wrapped almond paste in a freezer bag for up to six months.

BISKUTTINI TAR-RAHAL (VILLAGE BISCUITS)

(courtesy of Vicky Muscat)

Ingredients

4 cups sifted All Purpose Flour
2 cups sugar
4 eggs
½ tsp. Cloves
1 tbsp. Caraway seeds
1 tsp. Baking powder
3 tbsp. Marmalade
1 fresh lemon zest and juice.

Instructions: Preheat oven to 350⁰.

1. In a large bowl, beat sugar and eggs together.
2. Then slowly add the rest of the ingredients. Until fully mixed.
3. Place some loose flour on a plate to help form the balls, as the dough is quite sticky.
4. 1 tsp. at a time, place the dough on the plated loose flour. Roll them into balls. Then flatten them naqra——.
5. Place flattened balls on a baking tray lined with parchment paper.
6. Bake for about 15 to 20 minutes.
7. Enjoy!

Apply icing if desired.

QAQHAQ TAL GUNGLIEN (SESAME RINGS)

(courtesy of Mary Muscat)

Ingredients

6 cups flour
2 orange zest
1 tbsp. brown sugar
dash of cloves
4 eggs
dash of allspice
Juice of 2 oranges
Sesame seeds
1 stick of butter, melted
3 tsp. baking powder
1 tsp. anise seeds

Instructions

1. Mix flour and brown sugar.
2. Make a wheel in the center.
3. Add 4 eggs, juice of 2 oranges, and a stick of melted butter, and mix well.
4. Add 3 tsp. of baking powder and tsp. of anise seeds.
5. Add the zest of 2 oranges.
6. Add a dash of cloves and a dash of allspice.
7. Mix, and work with hands just enough to blend.
8. Roll into a long roll.
9. Cover with sesame seeds.
10. Cut into 6-inch-long pieces. Then shape as donuts.
11. Bake at 350F for 15-16 minutes.

FIGOLLI (EASTER COOKIE)

(courtesy of Maltese American Community Club)

<u>Dough</u>
Ingredients
1 ½ sticks margarine
3 tbsp. baking powder
1 cup sugar
½ tsp. salt
2 eggs
¾ cup milk
3 ½ cups sifted flour
1 tsp. vanilla

Instructions

1. Mix sugar, baking powder, salt, and margarine to a crumbled consistency.
2. Next, add all the wet ingredients and mix well. Let the dough stand for half an hour.

<u>Filling</u>
Ingredients
3 ½ cups ground almonds
½ cup water
4 oz sugar
½ bottle Almond Extract

Instructions

1. Mix sugar and water in a saucepan and bring to a boil.
2. Remove from stove and add almond extract.
3. Start adding the ground almond and stir, mix it well until the filling becomes thick and paste-like. If the filling becomes too runny, add some extra ground almonds to thicken the filling.

Continue >>

\>> **Continued**

<u>Royal Icing</u>

Ingredients

1 cup powdered sugar
warm water
1 egg white
food coloring (pink, green, and white are traditional colors)
lemon juice of 1 lemon

Instructions

1. Mix sugar, egg white, lemon juice, and warm water to a very thick consistency.
2. Place icing in a decorating bag and decorate figolli. Place a chocolate Easter egg on top.
3. You can also use sprinkles, M&M's, or jelly beans on top of the figolli.

<u>Glaze</u>

powdered sugar
water

Make sure it is thick but spreadable

Assembly

1. Preheat oven to 350F.
2. With a rolling pin, roll the dough to about a quarter inch thick.
3. Cut the dough with a cookie cutter.
4. Lay them on a sprayed baking sheet at least one inch apart.
5. With a teaspoon, spread the almond filling mixture on the cutout dough.
6. Repeat by rolling the dough and cutting out the shapes with the cookie cutter. Stacking the same shapes together.
7. Bake figolli until golden brown.
8. Let figolli cool before decorating. Decorate figolli with melted chocolate or the traditional royal icing.

GALLETTI (MALTESE CRACKER)

Ingredients

½ oz. yeast
5-6 oz. warm water
7 oz. flour
Pinch of salt
5 oz. semolina
½ lb. butter

Instructions

1. Put the yeast in water.
2. Combine the flour and salt. Pass through a sifter.
3. Add the semolina, and rub it in the butter.
4. Add the yeast and enough water until you have a pliable but rather dry dough, work a little dough at a time, keeping the rest in the refrigerator to stop the rising.
5. Roll out very thinly on a floured board and cut into rounds using a small cutter.
6. Prick each biscuit with a fork and lay it on a floured baking sheet.
7. Bake at 400F.
   Cool on a wire tray, when completely cool, store in an airtight tin.

IMQARET (DATE FILLED SNACK)

Ingredients

Dough
14 oz flour
3.5 oz cold butter cubed
1 tbsp orange flower water
1 tbsp sugar
½ tsp baking-power
4 tbsp of water
1 tsp aniseed liquor

Date Filling
14oz. pitted dates
Zest of an orange
1 tbsp. orange flower water
½ cup water
1 tsp. cloves
1 tsp cinnamon
1 tsp aniseed

Instructions

For The Dough

1. Add all the ingredients together, except the water, and combine everything. Start adding the water slowly and knead. Knead for a few minutes until you get a smooth dough.
2. Wrap the dough in plastic wrap and place it in the refrigerator for an hour or so.

For The Filling

1. Chop the dates into small pieces and place them in a bowl of water, just covering the dates, for about half an hour.

Continue >>

>> **Continued**

2. Remove the dates from the water and place them in a pot on low heat. Reserve the water and set it aside.
3. Together with the dates add all the other ingredients and cook on low heat. While constantly mixing add the water. Keep cooking on low until the dates break down and form a thick mixture. Place the paste in the refrigerator for about an hour.

Assembly

1. Divide the dough and the filling into four portions.
2. On a floured surface, roll each dough into a long rectangle about 19 ½ inches by 4-6 inches wide.
3. Layer the paste on the dough, about 10 balls, on one side, leaving a border. Fold the dough over and press gently.
4. Cut horizontally the diamond-shaped imqaret.

Fried Imqaret

1. Fill a large pot with corn oil. Fry in hot, deep-fried oil.
2. Cook the imqaret in small batches for a minute on each side. Drain on paper towels.

Baked Imqaret

1. Preheat oven to 350F. Line a baking tray with parchment paper and sprinkle some flour on top. Line the imqaret on the tray, leaving some space between them.
2. Bake for 20 minutes or until they are golden brown (makes about 30 snacks)

PUDINA TAL-HOBZ (BREAD PUDDING)

(courtesy of Doris Gauci-Attard)

Ingredients

1 ½ loaf Italian bread
1 cup of sultanas (raisin)
2 oz of margarine
2 tbsp. dark cocoa
4 oz. Sugar
Pinch of nutmeg
3 eggs
½ cup walnuts chopped up
2 oz grated lemon and orange peel
1 tsp. mixed spice
drop of vanilla extract
1 tsp. baking powder
drop of anise extract
1 can evaporated milk
1 drop of almond extract

Instructions

1. Cut the bread into small pieces, cover it in a bowl of water leave for an hour.
2. Drain the bread with your hands until dry.
3. Add the remaining ingredients to the bread.
4. Mix well using your fingers.
5. Grease a 9x12 baking dish with margarine and spread the mixture in it.
6. Bake in a 350F oven for about half an hour. Serve cold.

QAGHAG TAL-GHASEL (HONEY RING)

(courtesy of Pawla Gauci)

Ingredients

Pastry
3 lbs. self-rising flour
2 oz. margarine
½ cup sugar
Vanilla
½ cup evaporated milk
Orange & lemon **zest**
12 oz. water

Ghasel
2 cups water
2 can treacle (blackstrap molasses)
1 tin marmalade
Zest of lemon or orange
Lemon or orange juice
Some cloves

Instructions

1. Put all the filling ingredients in a saucepan and bring to a boil.
2. Continue cooking for a few seconds and leave to cool.
3. Rub the margarine into the flour and bind it with the yolks and a little water.
4. Leave the pastry to set for two hours before using. Roll out the pastry into long strips of 3x6 inches.
5. Put some filling in the middle, the whole length of the pastry, and fold the pastry.
6. Now, bring the two ends of the pastry together to form a ring.
7. Dust the baking pan with semolina.
8. Take a sharp knife and slit the pastry into different places.
9. Put the rings on the baking sheet and bake at 350F for 25 minutes.

XKUNVAT (CRUMPETS)

Ingredients

7 oz. flour
A little anisette
¾ oz. butter
A little water
2 egg yolks
Honey
1 oz. castor sugar
Oil

Instructions

1. Rub the flour and butter together.
2. Add the sugar, eggs, liqueur, and water, making a dough.
3. Leave to set for one hour.
4. Roll the pastry very thinly.
5. Using a pastry wheel, cut into half-inch strips.
6. Twist each strip into knots, drop them into boiling oil, fry till golden.
7. Drain from oil and put into a paper-lined serving dish. Sprinkle with honey.

Printed in Great Britain
by Amazon